James Russell Lowell

Under the Willows, and Other Poems

James Russell Lowell

Under the Willows, and Other Poems

ISBN/EAN: 9783744770675

Printed in Europe, USA, Canada, Australia, Japan

Cover: Foto ©Thomas Meinert / pixelio.de

More available books at **www.hansebooks.com**

UNDER THE WILLOWS

AND

OTHER POEMS.

First edition

BY

JAMES RUSSELL LOWELL.

BOSTON:
FIELDS, OSGOOD, & CO.,
SUCCESSORS TO TICKNOR AND FIELDS.
1869.

Entered according to Act of Congress, in the year 1868, by
JAMES RUSSELL LOWELL,
in the Clerk's Office of the District Court of the District of Massachusetts.

UNIVERSITY PRESS: WELCH, BIGELOW, & CO.,
CAMBRIDGE.

TO CHARLES ELIOT NORTON.

AGRO DOLCE.

THE wind is roistering out of doors,
   My windows shake and my chimney roars;
My Elmwood chimneys seem crooning to me,
As of old, in their moody, minor key,
And out of the past the hoarse wind blows,
As I sit in my arm-chair, and toast my toes.

"Ho! ho! nine-and-forty," they seem to sing,
"We saw you a little toddling thing,
We knew you child and youth and man,
A wonderful fellow to dream and plan,
With a great thing always to come, — who knows?
Well, well! 't is some comfort to toast one's toes.

"How many times have you sat at gaze
Till the mouldering fire forgot to blaze,

Shaping among the whimsical coals
Fancies and figures and shining goals!
What matters the ashes that cover those?
While hickory lasts you can toast your toes.

"O dream-ship-builder! where are they all,
Your grand three-deckers, deep-chested and tall,
That should crush the waves under canvas piles,
And anchor at last by the Fortunate Isles?
There's gray in your beard, the years turn foes,
While you muse in your arm-chair and toast your toes."

I sit and dream that I hear, as of yore,
My Elmwood chimneys' deep-throated roar;
If much be gone, there is much remains;
By the embers of loss I count my gains,
You and yours with the best, till the old hope glows
In the fanciful flame, as I toast my toes.

TO CHARLES ELIOT NORTON.

Instead of a fleet of broad-browed ships,
To send a child's armada of chips!
Instead of the great guns, tier on tier,
A freight of pebbles and grass-blades sere!
" Well, maybe more love with the less gift goes,"
I growl, as, half moody, I toast my toes.

[*⁎* No collection of the author's poems has been made since 1848, and some of those in this volume date back even farther than that. All but two of the shortest have been printed before, either wholly or in part. As the greater number, however, were published more than fifteen years ago, they will have, perhaps, something of novelty to most readers. A few pieces, more strictly comic, have been omitted, as out of keeping; and "Fitz Adam's Story," which some good friends will miss, is also left to stand over, because it belongs to a connected series, which, it is hoped, may be completed if the days should be propitious.]

CONTENTS.

	PAGE
UNDER THE WILLOWS	9
DARA	28
THE FIRST SNOW-FALL	32
THE SINGING LEAVES	35
SEA-WEED	41
THE FINDING OF THE LYRE	43
NEW-YEAR'S EVE. 1850.	45
FOR AN AUTOGRAPH	47
AL FRESCO	49
MASACCIO	55
WITHOUT AND WITHIN	58
GODMINSTER CHIMES	60
THE PARTING OF THE WAYS	63
ALADDIN	70
AN INVITATION	71
THE NOMADES	78
SELF-STUDY	82
PICTURES FROM APPLEDORE	84
THE WIND-HARP	104
AUF WIEDERSEHEN!	107
PALINODE	109
AFTER THE BURIAL	111
THE DEAD HOUSE	114
A MOOD	117

THE VOYAGE TO VINLAND	120
MAHMOOD THE IMAGE-BREAKER	135
INVITA MINERVA	138
THE FOUNTAIN OF YOUTH	141
YUSSOUF	153
THE DARKENED MIND	155
WHAT RABBI JEHOSHA SAID	157
ALL-SAINTS	159
A WINTER-EVENING HYMN TO MY FIRE	161
FANCY'S CASUISTRY	171
TO MR. JOHN BARTLETT	175
ODE TO HAPPINESS	178
VILLA FRANCA	184
THE MINER	189
GOLD EGG: A DREAM-FANTASY	192
A FAMILIAR EPISTLE TO A FRIEND	201
AN EMBER PICTURE	211
TO H. W. L.	214
THE NIGHTINGALE IN THE STUDY	216
IN THE TWILIGHT	220
THE FOOT-PATH	224
POEMS OF THE WAR.	
THE WASHERS OF THE SHROUD	231
TWO SCENES FROM THE LIFE OF BLONDEL	238
MEMORIÆ POSITUM	245
ON BOARD THE '76	250
ODE RECITED AT THE HARVARD COMMEMORATION	254
L'ENVOI. — TO THE MUSE	277

UNDER THE WILLOWS.

FRANK-HEARTED hostess of the field and wood,
    Gypsy, whose roof is every spreading tree,
June is the pearl of our New England year.
Still a surprisal, though expected long,
Her coming startles. Long she lies in wait,
Makes many a feint, peeps forth, draws coyly back,
Then, from some southern ambush in the sky,
With one great gush of blossom storms the world.
A week ago the sparrow was divine;
The bluebird, shifting his light load of song
From post to post along the cheerless fence,
Was as a rhymer ere the poet come;
But now, O rapture! sunshine winged and voiced,
Pipe blown through by the warm wild breath of the
    West
Shepherding his soft droves of fleecy cloud,

Gladness of woods, skies, waters, all in one,
The bobolink has come, and, like the soul
Of the sweet season vocal in a bird,
Gurgles in ecstasy we know not what
Save *June! Dear June! Now God be praised for June!*

May is a pious fraud of the almanac,
A ghastly parody of real Spring
Shaped out of snow and breathed with eastern wind;
Or if, o'er-confident, she trust the date,
And, with her handful of anemones,
Herself as shivery, steal into the sun,
The season need but turn his hourglass round,
And Winter suddenly, like crazy Lear,
Reels back, and brings the dead May in his arms,
Her budding breasts and wan dislustred front
With frosty streaks and drifts of his white beard
All overblown. Then, warmly walled with books,
While my wood-fire supplies the sun's defect,
Whispering old forest-sagas in its dreams,
I take my May down from the happy shelf
Where perch the world's rare song-birds in a row,

Waiting my choice to open with full breast,
And beg an alms of spring-time, ne'er denied
Indoors by vernal Chaucer, whose fresh woods
Throb thick with merle and mavis all the year.

July breathes hot, sallows the crispy fields,
Curls up the wan leaves of the lilac-hedge,
And every eve cheats us with show of clouds
That braze the horizon's western rim, or hang
Motionless, with heaped canvas drooping idly,
Like a dim fleet by starving men besieged,
Conjectured half, and half descried afar,
Helpless of wind, and seeming to slip back
Adown the smooth curve of the oily sea.

But June is full of invitations sweet,
Forth from the chimney's yawn and thrice-read
    tomes
To leisurely delights and sauntering thoughts
That brook no ceiling narrower than the blue.
The cherry, drest for bridal, at my pane
Brushes, then listens, *Will he come?* The bee,

All dusty as a miller, takes his toll
Of powdery gold, and grumbles. What a day
To sun me and do nothing! Nay, I think
Merely to bask and ripen is sometimes
The student's wiser business; the brain
That forages all climes to line its cells,
Ranging both worlds on lightest wings of wish,
Will not distil the juices it has sucked
To the sweet substance of pellucid thought,
Except for him who hath the secret learned
To mix his blood with sunshine, and to take
The winds into his pulses. Hush! 'T is he!
My oriole, my glance of summer fire,
Is come at last, and, ever on the watch,
Twitches the pack-thread I had lightly wound
About the bough to help his housekeeping, —
Twitches and scouts by turns, blessing his luck,
Yet fearing me who laid it in his way,
Nor, more than wiser we in our affairs,
Divines the providence that hides and helps.
Heave, ho! Heave, ho! he whistles as the twine
Slackens its hold; *once more, now!* and a flash

Lightens across the sunlight to the elm
Where his mate dangles at her cup of felt.
Nor all his booty is the thread; he trails
My loosened thought with it along the air,
And I must follow, would I ever find
The inward rhyme to all this wealth of life.

I care not how men trace their ancestry,
To ape or Adam; let them please their whim;
But I in June am midway to believe
A tree among my far progenitors,
Such sympathy is mine with all the race,
Such mutual recognition vaguely sweet
There is between us. Surely there are times
When they consent to own me of their kin,
And condescend to me, and call me cousin,
Murmuring faint lullabies of eldest time,
Forgotten, and yet dumbly felt with thrills
Moving the lips, though fruitless of the words.
And I have many a life-long leafy friend,
Never estranged nor careful of my soul,
That knows I hate the axe, and welcomes me

Within his tent as if I were a bird,
Or other free companion of the earth,
Yet undegenerate to the shifts of men.

Among them one, an ancient willow, spreads
Eight balanced limbs, springing at once all round
His deep-ridged trunk with upward slant diverse,
In outline like enormous beaker, fit
For hand of Jotun, where 'mid snow and mist
He holds unwieldy revel. This tree, spared,
I know not by what grace, — for in the blood
Of our New World subduers lingers yet
Hereditary feud with trees, they being
(They and the red-man most) our fathers' foes, —
Is one of six, a willow Pleiades,
The seventh fallen, that lean along the brink
Where the steep upland dips into the marsh,
Their roots, like molten metal cooled in flowing,
Stiffened in coils and runnels down the bank.
The friend of all the winds, wide-armed he towers
And glints his steely aglets in the sun,
Or whitens fitfully with sudden bloom

Of leaves breeze-lifted, much as when a shoal
Of devious minnows wheel from where a pike
Lurks balanced 'neath the lily-pads, and whirl
A rood of silver bellies to the day.

Alas! no acorn from the British oak
'Neath which slim fairies tripping wrought those
      rings
Of greenest emerald, wherewith fireside life
Did with the invisible spirit of Nature wed,
Was ever planted here! No darnel fancy
Might choke one useful blade in Puritan fields;
With horn and hoof the good old Devil came,
The witch's broomstick was not contraband,
But all that superstition had of fair,
Or piety of native sweet, was doomed.
And if there be who nurse unholy faiths,
Fearing their god as if he were a wolf
That snuffed round every home and was not seen,
There should be some to watch and keep alive
All beautiful beliefs. And such was that, —
By solitary shepherd first surmised

Under Thessalian oaks, loved by some maid
Of royal stirp, that silent came and vanished,
As near her nest the hermit thrush, nor dared
Confess a mortal name, — that faith which gave
A Hamadryad to each tree; and I
Will hold it true that in this willow dwells
The open-handed spirit, frank and blithe,
Of ancient Hospitality, long since,
With ceremonious thrift, bowed out of doors.

In June 't is good to lie beneath a tree
While the blithe season comforts every sense,
Steeps all the brain in rest, and heals the heart,
Brimming it o'er with sweetness unawares,
Fragrant and silent as that rosy snow
Wherewith the pitying apple-tree fills up
And tenderly lines some last-year robin's nest.
There muse I of old times, old hopes, old friends, —
Old friends! The writing of those words has borne
My fancy backward to the gracious past,
The generous past, when all was possible,
For all was then untried; the years between

Have taught some sweet, some bitter lessons, none
Wiser than this, — to spend in all things else,
But of old friends to be most miserly.
Each year to ancient friendships adds a ring,
As to an oak, and precious more and more,
Without deservingness or help of ours,
They grow, and, silent, wider spread, each year,
Their unbought ring of shelter or of shade.
Sacred to me the lichens on the bark,
Which Nature's milliners would scrape away;
Most dear and sacred every withered limb!
'T is good to set them early, for our faith
Pines as we age, and, after wrinkles come,
Few plant, but water dead ones with vain tears.

This willow is as old to me as life;
And under it full often have I stretched,
Feeling the warm earth like a thing alive,
And gathering virtue in at every pore
Till it possessed me wholly, and thought ceased,
Or was transfused in something to which thought
Is coarse and dull of sense. Myself was lost,

Gone from me like an ache, and what remained
Become a part of the universal joy.
My soul went forth, and, mingling with the tree,
Danced in the leaves; or, floating in the cloud,
Saw its white double in the stream below;
Or else, sublimed to purer ecstasy,
Dilated in the broad blue over all.
I was the wind that dappled the lush grass,
The tide that crept with coolness to its roots,
The thin-winged swallow skating on the air;
The life that gladdened everything was mine.
Was I then truly all that I beheld?
Or is this stream of being but a glass
Where the mind sees its visionary self,
As, when the kingfisher flits o'er his bay,
Across the river's hollow heaven below
His picture flits, — another, yet the same?
But suddenly the sound of human voice
Or footfall, like the drop a chemist pours,
Doth in opacous cloud precipitate
The consciousness that seemed but now dissolved
Into an essence rarer than its own,
And I am narrowed to myself once more.

For here not long is solitude secure,
Nor Fantasy left vacant to her spell.
Here, sometimes, in this paradise of shade,
Rippled with western winds, the dusty Tramp,
Seeing the treeless causey burn beyond,
Halts to unroll his bundle of strange food
And munch an unearned meal. I cannot help
Liking this creature, lavish Summer's bedesman,
Who from the almshouse steals when nights grow
    warm,
Himself his large estate and only charge,
To be the guest of haystack or of hedge,
Nobly superior to the household gear
That forfeits us our privilege of nature.
I bait him with my match-box and my pouch,
Nor grudge the uncostly sympathy of smoke,
His equal now, divinely unemployed.
Some smack of Robin Hood is in the man,
Some secret league with wild wood-wandering
    things;
He is our ragged Duke, our barefoot Earl,
By right of birth exonerate from toil,

Who levies rent from us his tenants all,
And serves the state by merely being. Here
The Scissors-grinder, pausing, doffs his hat,
And lets the kind breeze, with its delicate fan,
Winnow the heat from out his dank gray hair, —
A grimy Ulysses, a much-wandered man,
Whose feet are known to all the populous ways,
And many men and manners he hath seen,
Not without fruit of solitary thought.
He, as the habit is of lonely men, —
Unused to try the temper of their mind
In fence with others, — positive and shy,
Yet knows to put an edge upon his speech,
Pithily Saxon in unwilling talk.
Him I entrap with my long-suffering knife,
And, while its poor blade hums away in sparks,
Sharpen my wit upon his gritty mind,
In motion set obsequious to his wheel,
And in its quality not much unlike.

Nor wants my tree more punctual visitors.
The children, they who are the only rich,

Creating for the moment, and possessing
Whate'er they choose to feign, — for still with
    them
Kind Fancy plays the fairy godmother,
Strewing their lives with cheap material
For wingëd horses and Aladdin's lamps,
Pure elfin-gold, by manhood's touch profane
To dead leaves disenchanted, — long ago
Between the branches of the tree fixed seats,
Making an o'erturned box their table. Oft
The shrilling girls sit here between school hours,
And play at *What's my thought like?* while the
    boys,
With whom the age chivalric ever bides,
Pricked on by knightly spur of female eyes,
Climb high to swing and shout on perilous boughs,
Or, from the willow's armory equipped
With musket dumb, green banner, edgeless sword,
Make good the rampart of their tree-redoubt
'Gainst eager British storming from below,
And keep alive the tale of Bunker's Hill.
Here, too, the men that mend our village ways,

Vexing McAdam's ghost with pounded slate,
Their nooning take; much noisy talk they spend
On horses and their ills; and, as John Bull
Tells of Lord This or That, who was his friend,
So these make boast of intimacies long
With famous teams, and add large estimates,
By competition swelled from mouth to mouth,
Of how much they could draw, till one, ill pleased
To have his legend overbid, retorts:
"You take and stretch truck-horses in a string
From here to Long Wharf end, one thing I know,
Not heavy neither, they could never draw, —
Ensign's long bow!" Then laughter loud and long.
So they in their leaf-shadowed microcosm
Image the larger world; for wheresoe'er
Ten men are gathered, the observant eye
Will find mankind in little, as the stars
Glide up and set, and all the heavens revolve
In the small welkin of a drop of dew.

I love to enter pleasure by a postern,
Not the broad popular gate that gulps the mob;

To find my theatres in roadside nooks,
Where men are actors, and suspect it not;
Where Nature all unconscious works her will,
And every passion moves with human gait,
Unhampered by the buskin or the train.
Hating the crowd, where we gregarious men
Lead lonely lives, I love society,
Nor seldom find the best with simple souls
Unswerved by culture from their native bent,
The ground we meet on being primal man
And nearer the deep bases of our lives.

But O, half heavenly, earthly half, my soul,
Canst thou from those late ecstasies descend,
Thy lips still wet with the miraculous wine
That transubstantiates all thy baser stuff
To such divinity that soul and sense,
Once more commingled in their source, are lost, —
Canst thou descend to quench a vulgar thirst
With the mere dregs and rinsings of the world?
Well, if my nature find her pleasure so,
I am content, nor need to blush; I take

My little gift of being clean from God,
Not haggling for a better, holding it
Good as was ever any in the world,
My days as good and full of miracle.
I pluck my nutriment from any bush,
Finding out poison as the first men did
By tasting and then suffering, if I must.
Sometimes my bush burns, and sometimes it is
A leafless wilding shivering by the wall;
But I have known when winter barberries
Pricked the effeminate palate with surprise
Of savor whose mere harshness seemed divine.

O, benediction of the higher mood
And human-kindness of the lower! for both
I will be grateful while I live, nor question
The wisdom that hath made us what we are,
With such large range as from the alehouse bench
Can reach the stars and be with both at home.
They tell us we have fallen on prosy days,
Condemned to glean the leavings of earth's feast
Where gods and heroes took delight of old;

But though our lives, moving in one dull round
Of repetition infinite, become
Stale as a newspaper once read, and though
History herself, seen in her workshop, seem
To have lost the art that dyed those glorious panes,
Rich with memorial shapes of saint and sage,
That pave with splendor the Past's dusky aisles, —
Panes that enchant the light of common day
With colors costly as the blood of kings,
Until it edge our thought with hues ideal, —
Yet while the world is left, while nature lasts
And man the best of nature, there shall be
Somewhere contentment for these human hearts,
Some freshness, some unused material
For wonder and for song. I lose myself
In other ways where solemn guide-posts say,
This way to Knowledge, This way to Repose,
But here, here only, I am ne'er betrayed,
For every by-path leads me to my love.

God's passionless reformers, influences,
That purify and heal and are not seen,

Shall man say whence your virtue is, or how
Ye make medicinal the wayside weed?
I know that sunshine, through whatever rift,
How shaped it matters not, upon my walls
Paints discs as perfect-rounded as its source,
And, like its antitype, the ray divine,
However finding entrance, perfect still,
Repeats the image unimpaired of God.

We, who by shipwreck only find the shores
Of divine wisdom, can but kneel at first;
Can but exult to feel beneath our feet,
That long stretched vainly down the yielding deeps,
The shock and sustenance of solid earth;
Inland afar we see what temples gleam
Through immemorial stems of sacred groves,
And we conjecture shining shapes therein;
Yet for a space we love to wonder here
Among the shells and sea-weed of the beach.

So mused I once within my willow-tent
One brave June morning, when the bluff northwest,

Thrusting aside a dank and snuffling day
That made us bitter at our neighbors' sins,
Brimmed the great cup of heaven with sparkling
    cheer
And roared a lusty stave; the sliding Charles,
Blue toward the west, and bluer and more blue,
Living and lustrous as a woman's eyes
Look once and look no more, with southward curve
Ran crinkling sunniness, like Helen's hair
Glimpsed in Elysium, insubstantial gold;
From blossom-clouded orchards, far away
The bobolink tinkled; the deep meadows flowed
With multitudinous pulse of light and shade
Against the bases of the southern hills,
While here and there a drowsy island rick
Slept and its shadow slept; the wooden bridge
Thundered, and then was silent; on the roofs
The sun-warped shingles rippled with the heat;
Summer on field and hill, in heart and brain,
All life washed clean in this high tide of June.

DARA.

WHEN Persia's sceptre trembled in a hand
　　Wilted with harem-heats, and all the land
Was hovered over by those vulture ills
That snuff decaying empire from afar,
Then, with a nature balanced as a star,
Dara arose a shepherd of the hills.

He who had governed fleecy subjects well
Made his own village by the selfsame spell
Secure and quiet as a guarded fold;
Then, gathering strength by slow and wise degrees,
Under his sway, to neighbor villages
Order returned, and faith, and justice old.

Now when it fortuned that a king more wise
Endued the realm with brain and hands and eyes,

He sought on every side men brave and just;
And having heard our mountain shepherd's praise,
How he refilled the mould of elder days,
To Dara gave a satrapy in trust.

So Dara shepherded a province wide,
Nor in his viceroy's sceptre took more pride
Than in his crook before; but envy finds
More food in cities than on mountains bare;
And the frank sun of natures clear and rare
Breeds poisonous fogs in low and marish minds.

Soon it was hissed into the royal ear,
That, though wise Dara's province, year by year,
Like a great sponge, sucked wealth and plenty
    up,
Yet, when he squeezed it at the king's behest,
Some yellow drops, more rich than all the rest,
Went to the filling of his private cup.

For proof, they said, that, wheresoe'er he went,
A chest, beneath whose weight the camel bent,

Went with him; and no mortal eye had seen
What was therein, save only Dara's own;
But, when 't was opened, all his tent was known
To glow and lighten with heaped jewels' sheen.

The King set forth for Dara's province straight;
There, as was fit, outside the city's gate,
The viceroy met him with a stately train,
And there, with archers circled, close at hand,
A camel with the chest was seen to stand:
The King's brow reddened, for the guilt was plain.

"Open me here," he cried, "this treasure-chest!"
'T was done; and only a worn shepherd's vest
Was found therein. Some blushed and hung the head;
Not Dara; open as the sky's blue roof
He stood, and "O my lord, behold the proof
That I was faithful to my trust," he said.

"To govern men, lo all the spell I had!
My soul in these rude vestments ever clad

Still to the unstained past kept true and leal,
Still on these plains could breathe her mountain air,
And fortune's heaviest gifts serenely bear,
Which bend men from their truth and make them reel.

"For ruling wisely I should have small skill,
Were I not lord of simple Dara still;
That sceptre kept, I could not lose my way."
Strange dew in royal eyes grew round and bright,
And strained the throbbing lids; before 't was night
Two added provinces blest Dara's sway.

THE FIRST SNOW-FALL.

THE snow had begun in the gloaming,
    And busily all the night
Had been heaping field and highway
    With a silence deep and white.

Every pine and fir and hemlock
    Wore ermine too dear for an earl,
And the poorest twig on the elm-tree
    Was ridged inch deep with pearl.

From sheds new-roofed with Carrara
    Came Chanticleer's muffled crow,
The stiff rails were softened to swan's-down,
    And still fluttered down the snow.

I stood and watched by the window
    The noiseless work of the sky,

And the sudden flurries of snow-birds,
   Like brown leaves whirling by.

I thought of a mound in sweet Auburn
   Where a little headstone stood;
How the flakes were folding it gently,
   As did robins the babes in the wood.

Up spoke our own little Mabel,
   Saying, "Father, who makes it snow?"
And I told of the good All-father
   Who cares for us here below.

Again I looked at the snow-fall,
   And thought of the leaden sky
That arched o'er our first great sorrow,
   When that mound was heaped so high.

I remembered the gradual patience
   That fell from that cloud like snow,
Flake by flake, healing and hiding
   The scar of our deep-plunged woe.

And again to the child I whispered,
　"The snow that husheth all,
Darling, the merciful Father
　Alone can make it fall!"

Then, with eyes that saw not, I kissed her;
　And she, kissing back, could not know
That *my* kiss was given to her sister,
　Folded close under deepening snow.

THE SINGING LEAVES.

A BALLAD.

I.

"WHAT fairings will ye that I bring?"
    Said the King to his daughters three;
"For I to Vanity Fair am boun,
    Now say, what shall they be?"

Then up and spake the eldest daughter,
    That lady tall and grand:
"O, bring me pearls and diamonds great,
    And gold rings for my hand."

Thereafter spake the second daughter,
    That was both white and red:
"For me bring silks that will stand alone,
    And a gold comb for my head."

Then came the turn of the least daughter,
    That was whiter than thistle-down,

And among the gold of her blithesome hair
   Dim shone the golden crown.

"There came a bird this morning,
   And sang 'neath my bower eaves,
Till I dreamed, as his music made me,
   'Ask thou for the Singing Leaves.'"

Then the brow of the King swelled crimson
   With a flush of angry scorn:
"Well have ye spoken, my two eldest,
   And chosen as ye were born;

"But she like a thing of peasant race,
   That is happy binding the sheaves";
Then he saw her dead mother in her face,
   And said, "Thou shalt have thy leaves."

II.

He mounted and rode three days and nights
   Till he came to Vanity Fair,
And 't was easy to buy the gems and the silk,
   But no Singing Leaves were there.

Then deep in the greenwood rode he,
   And asked of every tree,
"O, if you have ever a Singing Leaf,
   I pray you to give it me!"

But the trees all kept their counsel,
   And never a word said they,
Only there sighed from the pine-tops
   A music of seas far away.

Only the pattering aspen
   Made a sound of growing rain,
That fell ever faster and faster,
   Then faltered to silence again.

"O, where shall I find a little foot-page
    That would win both hose and shoon,
And will bring to me the Singing Leaves
    If they grow under the moon?"

Then lightly turned him Walter the page,
    By the stirrup as he ran:
"Now pledge ye me the truesome word
    Of a king and gentleman,

"That you will give me the first, first thing
    You meet at your castle-gate,
And the Princess shall get the Singing Leaves,
    Or mine be a traitor's fate."

The King's head dropt upon his breast
    A moment, as it might be;
'T will be my dog, he thought, and said,
    "My faith I plight to thee."

Then Walter took from next his heart
    A packet small and thin,
"Now give you this to the Princess Anne,
    The Singing Leaves are therein."

III.

As the King rode in at his castle gate,
    A maiden to meet him ran,
And "Welcome, father!" she laughed and cried
    Together, the Princess Anne.

"Lo, here the Singing Leaves," quoth he,
    "And woe, but they cost me dear!"
She took the packet, and the smile
    Deepened down beneath the tear.

It deepened down till it reached her heart,
    And then gushed up again,
And lighted her tears as the sudden sun
    Transfigures the summer rain.

And the first Leaf, when it was opened,
    Sang: "I am Walter the page,
And the songs I sing 'neath thy window
    Are my only heritage."

And the second Leaf sang: "But in the land
   That is neither on earth or sea,
My lute and I are lords of more
   Than thrice this kingdom's fee."

And the third Leaf sang, "Be mine! Be mine!"
   And ever it sang, "Be mine!"
Then sweeter it sang and ever sweeter,
   And said, "I am thine, thine, thine!"

At the first Leaf she grew pale enough,
   At the second she turned aside,
At the third, 't was as if a lily flushed
   With a rose's red heart's tide.

"Good counsel gave the bird," said she,
   "I have my hope thrice o'er,
For they sing to my very heart," she said,
   "And it sings to them evermore."

She brought to him her beauty and truth,
   But and broad earldoms three,
And he made her queen of the broader lands
   He held of his lute in fee.

SEA-WEED.

NOT always unimpeded can I pray,
    Nor, pitying saint, thine intercession claim;
Too closely clings the burden of the day,
And all the mint and anise that I pay
But swells my debt and deepens my self-blame.

Shall I less patience have than Thou, who know
That Thou revisit'st all who wait for thee,
Nor only fill'st the unsounded deeps below,
But dost refresh with punctual overflow
The rifts where unregarded mosses be?

The drooping sea-weed hears, in night abyssed,
Far and more far the wave's receding shocks,
Nor doubts, for all the darkness and the mist,
That the pale shepherdess will keep her tryst,
And shoreward lead again her foam-fleeced flocks.

For the same wave that rims the Carib shore
With momentary brede of pearl and gold,
Goes hurrying thence to gladden with its roar
Lorn weeds bound fast on rocks of Labrador,
By love divine on one sweet errand rolled.

And, though Thy healing waters far withdraw,
I, too, can wait and feed on hope of Thee
And of the dear recurrence of Thy law,
Sure that the parting grace that morning saw
Abides its time to come in search of me.

THE FINDING OF THE LYRE.

THERE lay upon the ocean's shore
   What once a tortoise served to cover.
A year and more, with rush and roar,
The surf had rolled it over,
Had played with it, and flung it by,
As wind and weather might decide it,
Then tossed it high where sand-drifts dry
Cheap burial might provide it.

It rested there to bleach or tan,
The rains had soaked, the suns had burned it;
With many a ban the fisherman
Had stumbled o'er and spurned it;
And there the fisher-girl would stay,
Conjecturing with her brother
How in their play the poor estray
Might serve some use or other.

So there it lay, through wet and dry,
As empty as the last new sonnet,
Till by and by came Mercury,
And, having mused upon it,
"Why, here," cried he, "the thing of things
In shape, material, and dimension!
Give it but strings, and, lo, it sings,
A wonderful invention!"

So said, so done; the chords he strained,
And, as his fingers o'er them hovered,
The shell disdained a soul had gained,
The lyre had been discovered.
O empty world that round us lies,
Dead shell, of soul and thought forsaken,
Brought we but eyes like Mercury's,
In thee what songs should waken!

NEW-YEAR'S EVE. 1850.

THIS is the midnight of the century, — hark!
    Through aisle and arch of Godminster have
        gone
Twelve throbs that tolled the zenith of the dark,
And mornward now the starry hands move on;
"Mornward!" the angelic watchers say,
"Passed is the sorest trial;
No plot of man can stay
The hand upon the dial;
Night is the dark stem of the lily Day."

If we, who watched in valleys here below,
Toward streaks, misdeemed of morn, our faces
        turned
When volcan glares set all the east aglow, —
We are not poorer that we wept and yearned;

Though earth swing wide from God's intent,
And though no man nor nation
Will move with full consent
In heavenly gravitation,
Yet by one Sun is every orbit bent.

FOR AN AUTOGRAPH.

THOUGH old the thought and oft exprest,
'T is his at last who says it best, —
I 'll try my fortune with the rest.

Life is a leaf of paper white
Whereon each one of us may write
His word or two, and then comes night.

"Lo, time and space enough," we cry,
"To write an epic!" so we try
Our nibs upon the edge, and die.

Muse not which way the pen to hold,
Luck hates the slow and loves the bold,
Soon come the darkness and the cold.

FOR AN AUTOGRAPH.

Greatly begin! though thou have time
But for a line, be that sublime, —
Not failure, but low aim, is crime.

Ah, with what lofty hope we came!
But we forget it, dream of fame,
And scrawl, as I do here, a name.

AL FRESCO.

THE dandelions and buttercups
   Gild all the lawn; the drowsy bee
Stumbles among the clover-tops,
And summer sweetens all but me:
Away, unfruitful lore of books,
For whose vain idiom we reject
The soul's more native dialect,
Aliens among the birds and brooks,
Dull to interpret or conceive
What gospels lost the woods retrieve!
Away, ye critics, city-bred,
Who set man-traps of thus and so,
And in the first man's footsteps tread,
Like those who toil through drifted snow!
Away, my poets, whose sweet spell
Can make a garden of a cell!

I need ye not, for I to-day
Will make one long sweet verse of play.

Snap, chord of manhood's tenser strain!
To-day I will be a boy again;
The mind's pursuing element,
Like a bow slackened and unbent,
In some dark corner shall be leant.
The robin sings, as of old, from the limb!
The cat-bird croons in the lilac-bush;
Through the dim arbor, himself more dim,
Silently hops the hermit-thrush,
The withered leaves keep dumb for him;
The irreverent buccaneering bee
Hath stormed and rifled the nunnery
Of the lily, and scattered the sacred floor
With haste-dropt gold from shrine to door;
There, as of yore,
The rich, milk-tingeing buttercup
Its tiny polished urn holds up,
Filled with ripe summer to the edge,
The sun in his own wine to pledge;

And our tall elm, this hundredth year
Doge of our leafy Venice here,
Who, with an annual ring, doth wed
The blue Adriatic overhead,
Shadows with his palatial mass
The deep canals of flowing grass.

  O unestranged birds and bees!
O face of nature always true!
O never-unsympathizing trees!
O never-rejecting roof of blue,
Whose rash disherison never falls
On us unthinking prodigals,
Yet who convictest all our ill,
So grand and unappeasable!
Methinks my heart from each of these
Plucks part of childhood back again,
Long there imprisoned, as the breeze
Doth every hidden odor seize
Of wood and water, hill and plain.
Once more am I admitted peer
In the upper house of Nature here,

And feel through all my pulses run
The royal blood of breeze and sun.

Upon these elm-arched solitudes
No hum of neighbor toil intrudes;
The only hammer that I hear
Is wielded by the woodpecker,
The single noisy calling his
In all our leaf-hid Sybaris;
The good old time, close-hidden here,
Persists, a loyal cavalier,
While Roundheads prim, with point of fox,
Probe wainscot-chink and empty box;
Here no hoarse-voiced iconoclast
Insults thy statues, royal Past;
Myself too prone the axe to wield,
I touch the silver side of the shield
With lance reversed, and challenge peace,
A willing convert of the trees.

How chanced it that so long I tost
A cable's length from this rich coast,

AL FRESCO.

With foolish anchors hugging close
The beckoning weeds and lazy ooze,
Nor had the wit to wreck before
On this enchanted island's shore,
Whither the current of the sea,
With wiser drift, persuaded me?

O, might we but of such rare days
Build up the spirit's dwelling-place!
A temple of so Parian stone
Would brook a marble god alone,
The statue of a perfect life,
Far-shrined from earth's bestaining strife,
Alas! though such felicity
In our vext world here may not be,
Yet, as sometimes the peasant's hut
Shows stones which old religion cut
With text inspired, or mystic sign
Of the Eternal and Divine,
Torn from the consecration deep
Of some fallen nunnery's mossy sleep,
So, from the ruins of this day

Crumbling in golden dust away,
The soul one gracious block may draw,
Carved with some fragment of the law,
Which, set in life's uneven wall,
Old benedictions may recall,
And lure some nunlike thoughts to take
Their dwelling here for memory's sake.

MASACCIO.

(IN THE BRANCACCI CHAPEL.)

He came to Florence long ago,
  And painted here these walls, that shone
For Raphael and for Angelo,
With secrets deeper than his own,
Then shrank into the dark again,
And died, we know not how or when.

The shadows deepened, and I turned
Half sadly from the fresco grand;
"And is this," mused I, "all ye earned,
High-vaulted brain and cunning hand,
That ye to greater men could teach
The skill yourselves could never reach?"

"And who were they," I mused, "that wrought
Through pathless wilds, with labor long,

The highways of our daily thought?
Who reared those towers of earliest song
That lift us from the throng to peace
Remote in sunny silences?"

Out clanged the Ave Mary bells,
And to my heart this message came:
Each clamorous throat among them tells
What strong-souled martyrs died in flame
To make it possible that thou
Shouldst here with brother sinners bow.

Thoughts that great hearts once broke for, we
Breathe cheaply in the common air;
The dust we trample heedlessly
Throbbed once in saints and heroes rare,
Who perished, opening for their race
New pathways to the commonplace.

Henceforth, when rings the health to those
Who live in story and in song,

O nameless dead, who now repose
Safe in Oblivion's chambers strong,
One cup of recognition true
Shall silently be drained to you!

WITHOUT AND WITHIN.

MY coachman, in the moonlight there,
    Looks through the side-light of the door;
I hear him with his brethren swear,
    As I could do, — but only more.

Flattening his nose against the pane,
    He envies me my brilliant lot,
Breathes on his aching fists in vain,
    And dooms me to a place more hot.

He sees me in to supper go,
    A silken wonder by my side,
Bare arms, bare shoulders, and a row
    Of flounces, for the door too wide.

He thinks how happy is my arm
    'Neath its white-gloved and jewelled load;

WITHOUT AND WITHIN.

And wishes me some dreadful harm,
   Hearing the merry corks explode.

Meanwhile I inly curse the bore
   Of hunting still the same old coon,
And envy him, outside the door,
   In golden quiets of the moon.

The winter wind is not so cold
   As the bright smile he sees me win,
Nor the host's oldest wine so old
   As our poor gabble sour and thin.

I envy him the ungyved prance
   By which his freezing feet he warms,
And drag my lady's-chains and dance
   The galley-slave of dreary forms.

O, could he have my share of din,
   And I his quiet! — past a doubt
'T would still be one man bored within,
   And just another bored without.

GODMINSTER CHIMES.

WRITTEN IN AID OF A CHIME OF BELLS FOR CHRIST CHURCH, CAMBRIDGE.

GODMINSTER? Is it Fancy's play?
   I know not, but the word
Sings in my heart, nor can I say
   Whether 't was dreamed or heard;
Yet fragrant in my mind it clings
   As blossoms after rain,
And builds of half-remembered things
   This vision in my brain.

Through aisles of long-drawn centuries
   My spirit walks in thought,
And to that symbol lifts its eyes
   Which God's own pity wrought;
From Calvary shines the altar's gleam,
   The Church's East is there,

The Ages one great minster seem,
   That throbs with praise and prayer.

And all the way from Calvary down
   The carven pavement shows
Their graves who won the martyr's crown
   And safe in God repose;
The saints of many a warring creed
   Who now in heaven have learned
That all paths to the Father lead
   Where Self the feet have spurned.

And, as the mystic aisles I pace,
   By aureoled workmen built,
Lives ending at the Cross I trace
   Alike through grace and guilt;
One Mary bathes the blessed feet
   With ointment from her eyes,
With spikenard one, and both are sweet,
   For both are sacrifice.

Moravian hymn and Roman chant
   In one devotion blend,

To speak the soul's eternal want
   Of Him, the inmost friend;
One prayer soars cleansed with martyr fire,
   One choked with sinner's tears,
In heaven both meet in one desire,
   And God one music hears.

Whilst thus I dream, the bells clash out
   Upon the Sabbath air,
Each seems a hostile faith to shout,
   A selfish form of prayer;
My dream is shattered, yet who knows
   But in that heaven so near
These discords find harmonious close
   In God's atoning ear?

O chime of sweet Saint Charity,
   Peal soon that Easter morn
When Christ for all shall risen be,
   And in all hearts new-born!
That Pentecost when utterance clear
   To all men shall be given,
When all shall say *My Brother* here,
   And hear *My Son* in heaven!

THE PARTING OF THE WAYS.

WHO hath not been a poet? Who hath not,
With life's new quiver full of wingëd years,
Shot at a venture, and then, following on,
Stood doubtful at the Parting of the Ways?

There once I stood in dream, and as I paused,
Looking this way and that, came forth to me
The figure of a woman veiled, that said,
"My name is Duty, turn and follow me";
Something there was that chilled me in her voice;
I felt Youth's hand grow slack and cold in mine,
As if to be withdrawn, and I replied:
"O, leave the hot wild heart within my breast!
Duty comes soon enough, too soon comes Death;
This slippery globe of life whirls of itself,
Hasting our youth away into the dark;
These senses, quivering with electric heats,

Too soon will show, like nests on wintry boughs
Obtrusive emptiness, too palpable wreck,
Which whistling northwinds line with downy snow
Sometimes, or fringe with foliaged rime, in vain,
Thither the singing birds no more return."

Then glowed to me a maiden from the left,
With bosom half disclosed, and naked arms
More white and undulant than necks of swans;
And all before her steps an influence ran
Warm as the whispering South that opens buds
And swells the laggard sails of Northern May.
"I am called Pleasure, come with me!" she said,
Then laughed, and shook out sunshine from her hair,
Not only that, but, so it seemed, shook out
All memory too, and all the moonlit past,
Old loves, old aspirations, and old dreams,
More beautiful for being old and gone.

So we two went together; downward sloped
The path through yellow meads, or so I dreamed,
Yellow with sunshine and young green, but I

Saw naught nor heard, shut up in one close joy;
I only felt the hand within my own,
Transmuting all my blood to golden fire,
Dissolving all my brain in throbbing mist.

Suddenly shrank the hand; suddenly burst
A cry that split the torpor of my brain,
And as the first sharp thrust of lightning loosens
From the heaped cloud its rain, loosened my sense:
"Save me!" it thrilled; "O hide me! there is
    Death!
Death the divider, the unmerciful,
That digs his pitfalls under Love and Youth
And covers Beauty up in the cold ground;
Horrible Death! bringer of endless dark;
Let him not see me! hide me in thy breast!"
Thereat I strove to clasp her, but my arms
Met only what slipped crumbling down, and fell,
A handful of gray ashes, at my feet.

I would have fled, I would have followed back
That pleasant path we came, but all was changed;

Rocky the way, abrupt, and hard to find;
Yet I toiled on, and, toiling on, I thought,
"That way lies Youth, and Wisdom, and all Good;
For only by unlearning Wisdom comes
And climbing backward to diviner Youth;
What the world teaches profits to the world,
What the soul teaches profits to the soul,
Which then first stands erect with Godward face,
When she lets fall her pack of withered facts,
The gleanings of the outward eye and ear,
And looks and listens with her finer sense;
Nor Truth nor Knowledge cometh from without."

After long weary days I stood again
And waited at the Parting of the Ways;
Again the figure of a woman veiled
Stood forth and beckoned, and I followed now:
Down to no bower of roses led the path,
But through the streets of towns where chatter-
    ing Cold
Hewed wood for fires whose glow was owned and
    fenced,

Where Nakedness wove garments of warm wool
Not for itself; — or through the fields it led
Where Hunger reaped the unattainable grain,
Where Idleness enforced saw idle lands,
Leagues of unpeopled soil, the common earth,
Walled round with paper against God and Man.
"I cannot look," I groaned, "at only these;
The heart grows hardened with perpetual wont,
And palters with a feigned necessity,
Bargaining with itself to be content;
Let me behold thy face."
      The Form replied:
"Men follow Duty, never overtake;
Duty nor lifts her veil nor looks behind."
But, as she spake, a loosened lock of hair
Slipped from beneath her hood, and I, who looked
To see it gray and thin, saw amplest gold;
Not that dull metal dug from sordid earth,
But such as the retiring sunset flood
Leaves heaped on bays and capes of island cloud.
"O Guide divine," I prayed, "although not yet
I may repair the virtue which I feel

Gone out at touch of untuned things and foul
With draughts of Beauty, yet declare how soon!"

"Faithless and faint of heart," the voice returned,
"Thou see'st no beauty save thou make it first;
Man, Woman, Nature, each is but a glass
Where the soul sees the image of herself,
Visible echoes, offsprings of herself.
But, since thou need'st assurance of how soon,
Wait till that angel comes who opens all,
The reconciler, he who lifts the veil,
The reuniter, the rest-bringer, Death."

I waited, and methought he came; but how,
Or in what shape, I doubted, for no sign,
By touch or mark, he gave me as he passed;
Only I know a lily that I held
Snapt short below the head and shrivelled up;
Then turned my Guide and looked at me unveiled,
And I beheld no face of matron stern,
But that enchantment I had followed erst,

Only more fair, more clear to eye and brain,
Heightened and chastened by a household charm;
She smiled, and "Which is fairer," said her eyes,
"The hag's unreal Florimel or mine?"

ALADDIN.

When I was a beggarly boy,
  And lived in a cellar damp,
I had not a friend nor a toy,
  But I had Aladdin's lamp;
When I could not sleep for cold,
  I had fire enough in my brain,
And builded, with roofs of gold,
  My beautiful castles in Spain!

Since then I have toiled day and night,
  I have money and power good store,
But I'd give all my lamps of silver bright,
  For the one that is mine no more;
Take, Fortune, whatever you choose,
  You gave, and may snatch again;
I have nothing 't would pain me to lose,
  For I own no more castles in Spain!

AN INVITATION.

NINE years have slipt like hour-glass sand
    From life's still-emptying globe away,
Since last, dear friend, I clasped your hand,
And stood upon the impoverished land,
    Watching the steamer down the bay.

I held the token which you gave,
While slowly the smoke-pennon curled
O'er the vague rim 'tween sky and wave,
And shut the distance like a grave,
    Leaving me in the colder world.

The old worn world of hurry and heat,
The young, fresh world of thought and scope,
While you, where beckoning billows fleet
Climb far sky-beaches still and sweet,
    Sank wavering down the ocean-slope.

AN INVITATION.

You sought the new world in the old,
I found the old world in the new,
All that our human hearts can hold,
The inward world of deathless mould,
The same that Father Adam knew.

He needs no ship to cross the tide,
Who, in the lives about him, sees
Fair window-prospects opening wide
O'er history's fields on every side,
To Ind and Egypt, Rome and Greece.

Whatever moulds of various brain
E'er shaped the world to weal or woe,
Whatever empires' wax and wane,
To him that hath not eyes in vain,
Our village-microcosm can show.

Come back our ancient walks to tread,
Dear haunts of lost or scattered friends,
Old Harvard's scholar-factories red,
Where song and smoke and laughter sped
The nights to proctor-haunted ends.

Constant are all our former loves,
Unchanged the icehouse-girdled pond,
Its hemlock glooms, its shadowy coves,
Where floats the coot and never moves,
Its slopes of long-tamed green beyond.

Our old familiars are not laid,
Though snapt our wands and sunk our books;
They beckon, not to be gainsaid,
Where, round broad meads that mowers wade,
The Charles his steel-blue sickle crooks.

Where, as the cloudbergs eastward blow,
From glow to gloom the hillsides shift
Their plumps of orchard-trees arow,
Their lakes of rye that wave and flow,
Their snowy whiteweed's summer drift.

There have we watched the West unfurl
A cloud Byzantium newly born,
With flickering spires and domes of pearl,
And vapory surfs that crowd and curl
Into the sunset's Golden Horn.

There, as the flaming occident
Burned slowly down to ashes gray,
Night pitched o'erhead her silent tent,
And glimmering gold from Hesper sprent
Upon the darkened river lay,

Where a twin sky but just before
Deepened, and double swallows skimmed,
And, from a visionary shore,
Hung visioned trees, that, more and more
Grew dusk as those above were dimmed.

Then eastward saw we slowly grow
Clear-edged the lines of roof and spire,
While great elm-masses blacken slow,
And linden-ricks their round heads show
Against a flush of widening fire.

Doubtful at first and far away,
The moon-flood creeps more wide and wide;
Up a ridged beach of cloudy gray,
Curved round the east as round a bay,
It slips and spreads its gradual tide.

Then suddenly, in lurid mood,
The moon looms large o'er town and field
As upon Adam, red like blood,
'Tween him and Eden's happy wood,
Glared the commissioned angel's shield.

Or let us seek the seaside, there
To wander idly as we list,
Whether, on rocky headlands bare,
Sharp cedar-horns, like breakers, tear
The trailing fringes of gray mist,

Or whether, under skies full flown,
The brightening surfs, with foamy din,
Their breeze-caught forelocks backward blown,
Against the beach's yellow zone,
Curl slow, and plunge forever in.

And, as we watch those canvas towers
That lean along the horizon's rim,
"Sail on," I'll say; "may sunniest hours
Convoy you from this land of ours,
Since from my side you bear not him!"

For years thrice three, wise Horace said,
A poem rare let silence bind;
And love may ripen in the shade,
Like ours, for nine long seasons laid
In deepest arches of the mind.

Come back! Not ours the Old World's good,
The Old World's ill, thank God, not ours;
But here, far better understood,
The days enforce our native mood,
And challenge all our manlier powers.

Kindlier to me the place of birth
That first my tottering footsteps trod;
There may be fairer spots of earth,
But all their glories are not worth
The virtue of the native sod.

Thence climbs an influence more benign
Through pulse and nerve, through heart and brain;
Sacred to me those fibres fine
That first clasped earth. O, ne'er be mine
The alien sun and alien rain!

AN INVITATION.

These nourish not like homelier glows
Or waterings of familiar skies,
And nature fairer blooms bestows
On the heaped hush of wintry snows,
In pastures dear to childhood's eyes,

Than where Italian earth receives
The partial sunshine's ampler boons,
Where vines carve friezes 'neath the eaves,
And, in dark firmaments of leaves,
The orange lifts its golden moons.

THE NOMADES.

WHAT Nature makes in any mood
    To me is warranted for good,
Though long before I learned to see
She did not set us moral theses,
And scorned to have her sweet caprices
Strait-waistcoated in you or me.

I, who take root and firmly cling,
Thought fixedness the only thing;
Why Nature made the butterflies,
(Those dreams of wings that float and hover
At noon the slumberous poppies over),
Was something hidden from mine eyes,

Till once, upon a rock's brown bosom,
Bright as a thorny cactus-blossom,
I saw a butterfly at rest;
Then first of both I felt the beauty;

The airy whim, the grim-set duty,
Each from the other took its best.

Clearer it grew than winter sky
That Nature still had reasons why;
And, shifting sudden as a breeze,
My fancy found no satisfaction,
No antithetic sweet attraction,
So great as in the Nomades.

Scythians, with Nature not at strife,
Light Arabs of our complex life,
They build no houses, plant no mills
To utilize Time's sliding river,
Content that it flow waste forever,
If they, like it, may have their wills.

An hour they pitch their shifting tents
In thoughts, in feelings, and events;
Beneath the palm-trees, on the grass,
They sing, they dance, make love, and chatter,
Vex the grim temples with their clatter,
And make Truth's fount their looking-glass.

A picnic life; from love to love,
From faith to faith they lightly move,
And yet, hard-eyed philosopher,
The flightiest maid that ever hovered
To me your thought-webs fine discovered,
No lens to see them through like her.

So witchingly her finger-tips
To Wisdom, as away she trips,
She kisses, waves such sweet farewells
To Duty, as she laughs "To-morrow!"
That both from that mad contrast borrow
A perfectness found nowhere else.

The beach-bird on its pearly verge
Follows and flies the whispering surge,
While, in his tent, the rock-stayed shell
Awaits the flood's star-timed vibrations,
And both, the flutter and the patience,
The sauntering poet loves them well.

Fulfil so much of God's decree
As works its problem out in thee,

Nor dream that in thy breast alone
The conscience of the changeful seasons,
The Will that in the planets reasons
With Space-wide logic, has its throne.

Thy virtue makes not vice of mine,
Unlike, but none the less divine;
Thy toil adorns, not chides, my play;
Nature of sameness is so chary,
With such wild whim the freakish fairy
Picks presents for the christening-day.

SELF-STUDY.

A PRESENCE both by night and day,
   That made my life seem just begun,
Yet scarce a presence, rather say
The warning aureole of one.

And yet I felt it everywhere;
Walked I the woodland's aisles along,
It seemed to brush me with its hair;
Bathed I, I heard a mermaid's song.

How sweet it was! A buttercup
Could hold for me a day's delight,
A bird could lift my fancy up
To ether free from cloud or blight.

Who was the nymph? Nay, I will see,
Methought, and I will know her near;

SELF-STUDY.

If such, divined, her charm can be,
Seen and possessed, how triply dear!

So every magic art I tried,
And spells as numberless as sand,
Until, one evening, by my side
I saw her glowing fulness stand.

I turned to clasp her, but "Farewell,"
Parting she sighed, "we meet no more;
Not by my hand the curtain fell
That leaves you conscious, wise, and poor.

"Since you have found me out, I go;
Another lover I must find,
Content his happiness to know,
Nor strive its secret to unwind."

PICTURES FROM APPLEDORE.

I.

A HEAP of bare and splintery crags
Tumbled about by lightning and frost,
With rifts and chasms and storm-bleached jags,
That wait and growl for a ship to be lost;
No island, but rather the skeleton
Of a wrecked and vengeance-smitten one,
Where, æons ago, with half-shut eye,
The sluggish saurian crawled to die,
Gasping under titanic ferns;
Ribs of rock that seaward jut,
Granite shoulders and boulders and snags,
Round which, though the winds in heaven be shut,
The nightmared ocean murmurs and yearns,
Welters, and swashes, and tosses, and turns,
And the dreary black sea-weed lolls and wags;
Only rock from shore to shore,

Only a moan through the bleak clefts blown,
With sobs in the rifts where the coarse kelp shifts,
Falling and lifting, tossing and drifting,
And under all a deep, dull roar,
Dying and swelling forevermore, —
Rock and moan and roar alone,
And the dread of some nameless thing unknown,
These make Appledore.

These make Appledore by night:
Then there are monsters left and right;
Every rock is a different monster;
All you have read of, fancied, dreamed,
When you waked at night because you screamed,
There they lie for half a mile,
Jumbled together in a pile,
And (though you know they never once stir),
If you look long, they seem to be moving
Just as plainly as plain can be,
Crushing and crowding, wading and shoving
Out into the awful sea,
Where you can hear them snort and spout

With pauses between, as if they were listening,
Then tumult anon when the surf breaks glistening
In the blackness where they wallow about.

II.

All this you would scarcely comprehend,
Should you see the isle on a sunny day;
Then it is simple enough in its way, —
Two rocky bulges, one at each end,
With a smaller bulge and a hollow between;
Patches of whortleberry and bay;
Accidents of open green,
Sprinkled with loose slabs square and gray,
Like graveyards for ages deserted; a few
Unsocial thistles; an elder or two,
Foamed over with blossoms white as spray;
And on the whole island never a tree
Save a score of sumachs, high as your knee,
That crouch in hollows where they may,
(The cellars where once stood a village, men say,)

Huddling for warmth, and never grew
Tall enough for a peep at the sea;
A general dazzle of open blue;
A breeze always blowing and playing rat-tat
With the bow of the ribbon round your hat;
A score of sheep that do nothing but stare
Up or down at you everywhere;
Three or four cattle that chew the cud
Lying about in a listless despair;
A medrick that makes you look overhead
With short, sharp scream, as he sights his prey,
And, dropping straight and swift as lead,
Splits the water with sudden thud;—
This is Appledore by day.

A common island, you will say;
But stay a moment: only climb
Up to the highest rock of the isle,
Stand there alone for a little while,
And with gentle approaches it grows sublime,
Dilating slowly as you win
A sense from the silence to take it in.

So wide the loneness, so lucid the air,
The granite beneath you so savagely bare,
You well might think you were looking down
From some sky-silenced mountain's crown,
Whose far-down pines are wont to tear
Locks of wool from the topmost cloud.
Only be sure you go alone,
For Grandeur is inaccessibly proud,
And never yet has backward thrown
Her veil to feed the stare of a crowd;
To more than one was never shown
That awful front, nor is it fit
That she, Cothurnus-shod, stand bowed
Until the self-approving pit
Enjoy the gust of its own wit
In babbling plaudits cheaply loud;
She hides her mountains and her sea
From the harriers of scenery,
Who hunt down sunsets, and huddle and bay,
Mouthing and mumbling the dying day.

Trust me, 't is something to be cast

Face to face with one's Self at last,
To be taken out of the fuss and strife,
The endless clatter of plate and knife,
The bore of books and the bores of the street,
From the singular mess we agree to call Life,
Where that is best which the most fools vote is,
And to be set down on one's own two feet
So nigh to the great warm heart of God,
You almost seem to feel it beat
Down from the sunshine and up from the sod;
To be compelled, as it were, to notice
All the beautiful changes and chances
Through which the landscape flits and glances,
And to see how the face of common day
Is written all over with tender histories,
When you study it that intenser way
In which a lover looks at his mistress.

Till now you dreamed not what could be done
With a bit of rock and a ray of sun;
But look, how fade the lights and shades
Of keen bare edge and crevice deep!

How doubtfully it fades and fades,
And glows again, yon craggy steep,
O'er which, through color's dreamiest grades,
The yellow sunbeams pause and creep!
Now pink it blooms, now glimmers gray,
Now shadows to a filmy blue,
Tries one, tries all, and will not stay,
But flits from opal hue to hue,
And runs through every tenderest range
Of change that seems not to be change,
So rare the sweep, so nice the art,
That lays no stress on any part,
But shifts and lingers and persuades;
So soft that sun-brush in the west,
That asks no costlier pigments' aids,
But mingling knobs, flaws, angles, dints,
Indifferent of worst or best,
Enchants the cliffs with wraiths and hints
And gracious preludings of tints,
Where all seems fixed, yet all evades,
And indefinably pervades
Perpetual movement with perpetual rest!

III.

Away northeast is Boone Island light;
You might mistake it for a ship,
Only it stands too plumb upright,
And like the others does not slip
Behind the sea's unsteady brink;
Though, if a cloud-shade chance to dip
Upon it a moment, 't will suddenly sink,
Levelled and lost in the darkened main,
Till the sun builds it suddenly up again,
As if with a rub of Aladdin's lamp.
On the main-land you see a misty camp
Of mountains pitched tumultuously:
That one looming so long and large
Is Saddleback, and that point you see
Over yon low and rounded marge,
Like the boss of a sleeping giant's targe
Laid over his breast, is Ossipee;
That shadow there may be Kearsarge;
That must be Great Haystack; I love these names,

Wherewith the lonely farmer tames
Nature to mute companionship
With his own mind's domestic mood,
And strives the surly world to clip
In the arms of familiar habitude.
'T is well he could not contrive to make
A Saxon of Agamenticus:
He glowers there to the north of us,
Wrapt in his blanket of blue haze,
Unconvertibly savage, and scorns to take
The white man's baptism or his ways.
Him first on shore the coaster divines
Through the early gray, and sees him shake
The morning mist from his scalp-lock of pines;
Him first the skipper makes out in the west,
Ere the earliest sunstreak shoots tremulous,
Plashing with orange the palpitant lines
Of mutable billow, crest after crest,
And murmurs *Agamenticus!*
As if it were the name of a saint.
But is that a mountain playing cloud,
Or a cloud playing mountain, just there, so faint?

Look along over the low right shoulder
Of Agamenticus into that crowd
Of brassy thunderheads behind it;
Now you have caught it, but, ere you are older
By half an hour, you will lose it and find it
A score of times; while you look 't is gone,
And, just as you 've given it up, anon
It is there again, till your weary eyes
Fancy they see it waver and rise,
With its brother clouds; it is Agiochook,
There if you seek not, and gone if you look,
Ninety miles off as the eagle flies.

But mountains make not all the shore
The main-land shows to Appledore;
Eight miles the heaving water spreads
To a long low coast with beaches and heads
That run through unimagined mazes,
As the lights and shades and magical hazes
Put them away or bring them near,
Shimmering, sketched out for thirty miles
Between two capes that waver like threads,

And sink in the ocean, and reappear,
Crumbled and melted to little isles,
With filmy trees, that seem the mere
Half-fancies of drowsy atmosphere;
And see the beach there, where it is
Flat as a threshing-floor, beaten and packed
With the flashing flails of weariless seas,
How it lifts and looms to a precipice,
O'er whose square front, a dream, no more,
The steepened sand-stripes seem to pour,
A murmurless vision of cataract;
You almost fancy you hear a roar,
Fitful and faint from the distance wandering;
But 't is only the blind old ocean maundering,
Raking the shingle to and fro,
Aimlessly clutching and letting go
The kelp-haired sedges of Appledore,
Slipping down with a sleepy forgetting,
And anon his ponderous shoulder setting,
With a deep, hoarse pant against Appledore.

IV.

Eastward as far as the eye can see,
Still eastward, eastward, endlessly,
The sparkle and tremor of purple sea
That rises before you, a flickering hill,
On and on to the shut of the sky,
And beyond, you fancy it sloping until
The same multitudinous throb and thrill
That vibrate under your dizzy eye
In ripples of orange and pink are sent
Where the poppied sails doze on the yard,
And the clumsy junk and proa lie
Sunk deep with precious woods and nard,
'Mid the palmy isles of the Orient.

Those leaning towers of clouded white
On the farthest brink of doubtful ocean,
That shorten and shorten out of sight,
Yet seem on the selfsame spot to stay,
Receding with a motionless motion,
Fading to dubious films of gray,

Lost, dimly found, then vanished wholly,
Will rise again, the great world under,
First films, then towers, then high-heaped clouds,
Whose nearing outlines sharpen slowly
Into tall ships with cobweb shrouds,
That fill long Mongol eyes with wonder,
Crushing the violet wave to spray
Past some low headland of Cathay; —
What was that sigh which seemed so near,
Chilling your fancy to the core?
'T is only the sad old sea you hear,
That seems to seek forevermore
Something it cannot find, and so,
Sighing, seeks on, and tells its woe
To the pitiless breakers of Appledore.

V.

How looks Appledore in a storm?
  I have seen it when its crags seemed frantic,
  Butting against the mad Atlantic,

When surge on surge would heap enorme,
    Cliffs of emerald topped with snow,
    That lifted and lifted, and then let go
A great white avalanche of thunder,
    A grinding, blinding, deafening ire
Monadnock might have trembled under;
    And the island, whose rock-roots pierce below
    To where they are warmed with the central fire,
You could feel its granite fibres racked,
    As it seemed to plunge with a shudder and thrill
    Right at the breast of the swooping hill,
And to rise again, snorting a cataract
Of rage-froth from every cranny and ledge,
    While the sea drew its breath in hoarse and deep,
And the next vast breaker curled its edge,
    Gathering itself for a mightier leap.

North, east, and south there are reefs and breakers
    You would never dream of in smooth weather,
That toss and gore the sea for acres,
    Bellowing and gnashing and snarling together;
Look northward, where Duck Island lies,

And over its crown you will see arise,
Against a background of slaty skies,
  A row of pillars still and white,
  That glimmer, and then are out of sight,
As if the moon should suddenly kiss,
  While you crossed the gusty desert by night,
The long colonnades of Persepolis;
Look southward for White Island light,
  The lantern stands ninety feet o'er the tide;
There is first a half-mile of tumult and fight,
Of dash and roar and tumble and fright,
  And surging bewilderment wild and wide,
Where the breakers struggle left and right,
  Then a mile or more of rushing sea,
And then the light-house slim and lone;
And whenever the weight of ocean is thrown
Full and fair on White Island head,
  A great mist-jotun you will see
  Lifting himself up silently
High and huge o'er the light-house top,
With hands of wavering spray outspread,
  Groping after the little tower,

That seems to shrink and shorten and cower,
Till the monster's arms of a sudden drop,
  And silently and fruitlessly
  He sinks again into the sea.

You, meanwhile, where drenched you stand,
  Awaken once more to the rush and roar,
And on the rock-point tighten your hand,
As you turn and see a valley deep,
  That was not there a moment before,
Suck rattling down between you and a heap
  Of toppling billow, whose instant fall
  Must sink the whole island once for all,
Or watch the silenter, stealthier seas
  Feeling their way to you more and more;
If they once should clutch you high as the knees,
They would whirl you down like a sprig of kelp,
Beyond all reach of hope or help; —
  And such in a storm is Appledore.

VI.

'T is the sight of a lifetime to behold
The great shorn sun as you see it now,
Across eight miles of undulant gold
That widens landward, weltered and rolled,
With freaks of shadow and crimson stains;
To see the solid mountain brow
As it notches the disk, and gains and gains
Until there comes, you scarce know when,
A tremble of fire o'er the parted lips
Of cloud and mountain, which vanishes, — then
From the body of day the sun-soul slips
And the face of earth darkens; but now the strips
Of western vapor, straight and thin,
From which the horizon's swervings win
A grace of contrast, take fire and burn
Like splinters of touchwood, whose edges a mould
Of ashes o'erfeathers; northward turn
For an instant, and let your eye grow cold
On Agamenticus, and when once more

You look, 't is as if the land-breeze, growing,
From the smouldering brands the film were blowing,
And brightening them down to the very core;
Yet they momently cool and dampen and deaden,
The crimson turns golden, the gold turns leaden,
Hardening into one black bar
O'er which, from the hollow heaven afar,
Shoots a splinter of light like diamond,
Half seen, half fancied; by and by,
Beyond whatever is most beyond
In the uttermost waste of desert sky,
Grows a star;
And over it, visible spirit of dew, —
Ah, stir not, speak not, hold your breath,
Or surely the miracle vanisheth, —
The new moon, tranced in unspeakable blue!
No frail illusion; this were true,
Rather, to call it the canoe
Hollowed out of a single pearl,
That floats us from the Present's whirl
Back to those beings which were ours,

When wishes were winged things like powers!
Call it not light, that mystery tender,
Which broods upon the brooding ocean,
That flush of ecstasied surrender
To indefinable emotion,
That glory, mellower than a mist
Of pearl dissolved with amethyst,
Which rims Square Rock, like what they paint
Of mitigated heavenly splendor
Round the stern forehead of a Saint!

No more a vision, reddened, largened,
The moon dips toward her mountain nest,
And, fringing it with palest argent,
Slow sheathes herself behind the margent
Of that long cloud-bar in the West,
Whose nether edge, erelong, you see
The silvery chrism in turn anoint,
And then the tiniest rosy point
Touched doubtfully and timidly
Into the dark blue's chilly strip,
As some mute, wondering thing below,

Awakened by the thrilling glow,
Might, looking up, see Dian dip
One lucent foot's delaying tip
In Latmian fountains long ago.

Knew you what silence was before?
Here is no startle of dreaming bird
That sings in his sleep, or strives to sing;
Here is no sough of branches stirred,
Nor noise of any living thing,
Such as one hears by night on shore;
Only, now and then, a sigh,
With fickle intervals between,
Sometimes far, and sometimes nigh,
Such as Andromeda might have heard,
And fancied the huge sea-beast unseen
Turning in sleep; it is the sea
That welters and wavers uneasily
Round the lonely reefs of Appledore.

THE WIND-HARP.

I TREASURE in secret some long, fine hair
   Of tenderest brown, but so inwardly golden
I half used to fancy the sunshine there,
So shy, so shifting, so waywardly rare,
  Was only caught for the moment and holden
While I could say *Dearest!* and kiss it, and then
In pity let go to the summer again.

I twisted this magic in gossamer strings
   Over a wind-harp's Delphian hollow;
Then called to the idle breeze that swings
All day in the pine-tops, and clings, and sings
  'Mid the musical leaves, and said, "O, follow
The will of those tears that deepen my words,
And fly to my window to waken these chords."

So they trembled to life, and, doubtfully
   Feeling their way to my sense, sang, "Say
     whether

They sit all day by the greenwood tree,
The lover and loved, as it wont to be,
  When we"——but grief conquered, and all
    together
They swelled such weird murmur as haunts a
    shore
Of some planet dispeopled,—"Nevermore"!

Then from deep in the past, as seemed to me,
  The strings gathered sorrow and sang forsaken,
"One lover still waits 'neath the greenwood tree,
But 't is dark," and they shuddered, "where lieth
    she
  Dark and cold! Forever must one be taken?"
But I groaned, "O harp of all ruth bereft,
This Scripture is sadder,—'the other left'!"

There murmured, as if one strove to speak,
  And tears came instead; then the sad tones
    wandered
And faltered among the uncertain chords
In a troubled doubt between sorrow and words;

At last with themselves they questioned and
    pondered,
"Hereafter?—who knoweth?" and so they sighed
Down the long steps that lead to silence and died.

AUF WIEDERSEHEN!

SUMMER.

THE little gate was reached at last,
   Half hid in lilacs down the lane;
She pushed it wide, and, as she past,
A wistful look she backward cast,
   And said, — "*Auf wiedersehen!*"

With hand on latch, a vision white
   Lingered reluctant, and again
Half doubting if she did aright,
Soft as the dews that fell that night,
   She said, — "*Auf wiedersehen!*"

The lamp's clear gleam flits up the stair;
   I linger in delicious pain;
Ah, in that chamber, whose rich air
To breathe in thought I scarcely dare,
   Thinks she, — "*Auf wiedersehen!*"

AUF WIEDERSEHEN.

'T is thirteen years; once more I press
  The turf that silences the lane;
I hear the rustle of her dress,
I smell the lilacs, and — ah, yes,
  I hear "*Auf wiedersehen!*"

Sweet piece of bashful maiden art!
  The English words had seemed too fain,
But these — they drew us heart to heart,
Yet held us tenderly apart;
  She said, "*Auf wiedersehen!*"

PALINODE.

AUTUMN.

STILL thirteen years: 't is autumn now
   On field and hill, in heart and brain;
The naked trees at evening sough;
The leaf to the forsaken bough
   Sighs not, — "We meet again!"

Two watched yon oriole's pendent dome,
   That now is void, and dank with rain,
And one, — O, hope more frail than foam!
The bird to his deserted home
   Sings not, — "We meet again!"

The loath gate swings with rusty creak;
   Once, parting there, we played at pain;
There came a parting, when the weak

And fading lips essayed to speak
   Vainly, — "We meet again!"

Somewhere is comfort, somewhere faith,
   Though thou in outer dark remain;
One sweet, sad voice ennobles death,
And still, for eighteen centuries saith
   Softly, — "Ye meet again!"

If earth another grave must bear,
   Yet heaven hath won a sweeter strain,
And something whispers my despair,
That, from an orient chamber there,
   Floats down, "We meet again!"

AFTER THE BURIAL.

YES, Faith is a goodly anchor;
    When skies are sweet as a psalm,
At the bows it lolls so stalwart,
In bluff, broad-shouldered calm.

And when over breakers to leeward
The tattered surges are hurled,
It may keep our head to the tempest,
With its grip on the base of the world.

But, after the shipwreck, tell me
What help in its iron thews,
Still true to the broken hawser,
Deep down among sea-weed and ooze?

In the breaking gulfs of sorrow,
When the helpless feet stretch out

And find in the deeps of darkness
No footing so solid as doubt,

Then better one spar of Memory,
One broken plank of the Past,
That our human heart may cling to,
Though hopeless of shore at last!

To the spirit its splendid conjectures,
To the flesh its sweet despair,
Its tears o'er the thin-worn locket
With its anguish of deathless hair!

Immortal? I feel it and know it,
Who doubts it of such as she?
But that is the pang's very secret,—
Immortal away from me.

There's a narrow ridge in the graveyard
Would scarce stay a child in his race,
But to me and my thought it is wider
Than the star-sown vague of Space.

AFTER THE BURIAL.

Your logic, my friend, is perfect,
Your morals most drearily true;
But, since the earth clashed on *her* coffin,
I keep hearing that, and not you.

Console if you will, I can bear it;
'T is a well-meant alms of breath;
But not all the preaching since Adam
Has made Death other than Death.

It is pagan; but wait till you feel it, —
That jar of our earth, that dull shock
When the ploughshare of deeper passion
Tears down to our primitive rock.

Communion in spirit! Forgive me,
But I, who am earthy and weak,
Would give all my incomes from dreamland
For a touch of her hand on my cheek.

That little shoe in the corner,
So worn and wrinkled and brown,
With its emptiness confutes you,
And argues your wisdom down.

THE DEAD HOUSE.

HERE once my step was quickened,
    Here beckoned the opening door,
And welcome thrilled from the threshold
    To the foot it had known before.

A glow came forth to meet me
    From the flame that laughed in the grate,
And shadows adance on the ceiling,
    Danced blither with mine for a mate.

"I claim you, old friend," yawned the arm-chair,
    "This corner, you know, is your seat";
"Rest your slippers on me," beamed the fender,
    "I brighten at touch of your feet."

"We know the practised finger,"
    Said the books, "that seems like brain";

And the shy page rustled the secret
   It had kept till I came again.

Sang the pillow, "My down once quivered
   On nightingales' throats that flew
Through moonlit gardens of Hafiz
   To gather quaint dreams for you."

Ah me, where the Past sowed heart's-ease,
   The Present plucks rue for us men!
I come back: that scar unhealing
   Was not in the churchyard then.

But, I think, the house is unaltered,
   I will go and beg to look
At the rooms that were once familiar
   To my life as its bed to a brook.

Unaltered! Alas for the sameness
   That makes the change but more!
'T is a dead man I see in the mirrors,
   'T is his tread that chills the floor!

To learn such a simple lesson,
   Need I go to Paris and Rome,
That the many make the household,
   But only one the home?

'T was just a womanly presence,
   An influence unexprest,
But a rose she had worn, on my grave-sod
   Were more than long life with the rest!

'T was a smile, 't was a garment's rustle,
   'T was nothing that I can phrase,
But the whole dumb dwelling grew conscious,
   And put on her looks and ways.

Were it mine I would close the shutters,
   Like lids when the life is fled,
And the funeral fire should wind it,
   This corpse of a home that is dead.

For it died that autumn morning
   When she, its soul, was borne
To lie all dark on the hillside
   That looks over woodland and corn.

A MOOD.

PINE in the distance,
　　Patient through sun or rain,
Meeting with graceful persistence,
With yielding but rooted resistance,
The northwind's wrench and strain,
No memory of past existence
Brings thee pain;
Right for the zenith heading,
Friendly with heat or cold,
Thine arms to the influence spreading
Of the heavens, just from of old,
Thou only aspirest the more,
Unregretful the old leaves shedding
That fringed thee with music before,
And deeper thy roots embedding
In the grace and the beauty of yore;
Thou sigh'st not, " Alas, I am older,

The green of last summer is sear!"
But loftier, hopefuller, bolder,
Wins broader horizons each year.

To me 't is not cheer thou art singing:
There 's a sound of the sea,
O mournful tree,
In thy boughs forever clinging,
And the far-off roar
Of waves on the shore
A shattered vessel flinging.

As thou musest still of the ocean
On which thou must float at last,
And seem'st to foreknow
The shipwreck's woe
And the sailor wrenched from the broken mast,
Do I, in this vague emotion,
This sadness that will not pass,
Though the air throbs with wings,
And the field laughs and sings,
Do I forebode, alas!

The ship-building longer and wearier,
The voyage's struggle and strife,
And then the darker and drearier
Wreck of a broken life?

THE VOYAGE TO VINLAND.

I.

BIÖRN'S BECKONERS.

NOW Biörn, the son of Heriulf, had ill days
  Because the heart within him seethed with
    blood
That would not be allayed with any toil,
Whether of war or hunting or the oar,
But was anhungered for some joy untried:
For the brain grew not weary with the limbs,
But, while they slept, still hammered like a Troll,
Building all night a bridge of solid dream
Between him and some purpose of his soul,
Or will to find a purpose. With the dawn
The sleep-laid timbers, crumbled to soft mist,
Denied all foothold. But the dream remained,
And every night with yellow-bearded kings
His sleep was haunted, — mighty men of old,
Once young as he, now ancient like the gods,
And safe as stars in all men's memories.

Strange sagas read he in their sea-blue eyes
Cold as the sea, grandly compassionless;
Like life, they made him eager and then mocked.
Nay, broad awake, they would not let him be;
They shaped themselves gigantic in the mist,
They rose far-beckoning in the lamps of heaven,
They whispered invitation in the winds,
And breath came from them, mightier than the wind,
To strain the lagging sails of his resolve,
Till that grew passion which before was wish,
And youth seemed all too costly to be staked
On the soiled cards wherewith men played their game,
Letting Time pocket up the larger life,
Lost with base gain of raiment, food, and roof.
"What helpeth lightness of the feet?" they said,
"Oblivion runs with swifter foot than they;
Or strength of sinew? New men come as strong,
And those sleep nameless; or renown in war?
Swords grave no name on the long-memoried rock
But moss shall hide it; they alone who wring
Some secret purpose from the unwilling gods

Survive in song for yet a little while
To vex, like us, the dreams of later men,
Ourselves a dream, and dreamlike all we did."

II.

THORWALD'S LAY.

So Biörn went comfortless but for his thought,
And by his thought the more discomforted,
Till Eric Thurlson kept his Yule-tide feast:
And thither came he, called among the rest,
Silent, lone-minded, a church-door to mirth:
But, ere deep draughts forbade such serious song
As the grave Skald might chant, nor after blush,
Then Eric looked at Thorwald, where he sat,
Mute as a cloud amid the stormy hall,
And said: "O Skald, sing now an olden song,
Such as our fathers heard who led great lives;
And, as the bravest on a shield is borne
Along the waving host that shouts him king,
So rode their thrones upon the thronging seas!"

Then the old man arose; white-haired he stood,
White-bearded, and with eyes that looked afar
From their still region of perpetual snow,
Beyond the little smokes and stirs of men:
His head was bowed with gathered flakes of years,
As winter bends the sea-foreboding pine,
But something triumphed in his brow and eye,
Which whoso saw it could not see and crouch:
Loud rang the emptied beakers as he mused,
Brooding his eyried thoughts; then, as an eagle
Circles smooth-winged above the wind-vexed woods,
So wheeled his soul into the air of song
High o'er the stormy hall; and thus he sang:
" The fletcher for his arrow-shaft picks out
Wood closest-grained, long-seasoned, straight as
    light;
And from a quiver full of such as these
The wary bowman, matched against his peers,
Long doubting, singles yet once more the best.
Who is it needs such flawless shafts as Fate?
What archer of his arrows is so choice,
Or hits the white so surely? They are men,

The chosen of her quiver; nor for her
Will every reed suffice, or cross-grained stick
At random from life's vulgar fagot plucked:
Such answer household ends; but she will have
Souls straight and clear, of toughest fibre, sound
Down to the heart of heart; from these she strips
All needless stuff, all sapwood, seasons them,
From circumstance untoward feathers plucks
Crumpled and cheap, and barbs with iron will:
The hour that passes is her quiver-boy;
When she draws bow, 't is not across the wind,
Nor 'gainst the sun her haste-snatched arrow sings,
For sun and wind have plighted faith to her:
Ere men have heard the sinew twang, behold
In the butt's heart her trembling messenger!

"The song is old and simple that I sing;
But old and simple are despised as cheap,
Though hardest to achieve of human things:
Good were the days of yore, when men were tried
By ring of shields, as now by ring of words;
But while the gods are left, and hearts of men,

And unlocked ocean, still the days are good.
Still o'er the earth hastes Opportunity,
Seeking the hardy soul that seeks for her.
Be not abroad, nor deaf with household cares
That chatter loudest as they mean the least;
Swift-willed is thrice-willed; late means nevermore;
Impatient is her foot, nor turns again."

He ceased; upon his bosom sank his beard
Sadly, as one who oft had seen her pass
Nor stayed her: and forthwith the frothy tide
Of interrupted wassail roared along;
But Biörn, the son of Heriulf, sat apart
Musing, and, with his eyes upon the fire,
Saw shapes of arrows, lost as soon as seen.
"A ship," he muttered, "is a wingëd bridge
That leadeth every way to man's desire,
And ocean the wide gate to manful luck";
And then with that resolve his heart was bent,
Which, like a humming shaft, through many a stripe
Of day and night, across the unpathwayed seas
Shot the brave prow that cut on Vinland sands
The first rune in the Saga of the West.

III.

GUDRIDA'S PROPHECY.

Four weeks they sailed, a speck in sky-shut seas,
Life, where was never life that knew itself,
But tumbled lubber-like in blowing whales;
Thought, where the like had never been before
Since Thought primeval brooded the abyss;
Alone as men were never in the world.
They saw the icy foundlings of the sea,
White cliffs of silence, beautiful by day,
Or looming, sudden-perilous, at night
In monstrous hush; or sometimes in the dark
The waves broke ominous with paly gleams
Crushed by the prow in sparkles of cold fire.
Then came green stripes of sea that promised land
But brought it not, and on the thirtieth day
Low in the West were wooded shores like cloud.
They shouted as men shout with sudden hope;
But Biörn was silent, such strange loss there is
Between the dream's fulfilment and the dream,

Such sad abatement in the goal attained.
Then Gudrida, that was a prophetess,
Rapt with strange influence from Atlantis, sang:
Her words: the vision was the dreaming shore's.

    Looms there the New Land:
    Locked in the shadow
    Long the gods shut it,
    Niggards of newness
    They, the o'er-old.

    Little it looks there,
    Slim as a cloud-streak;
    It shall fold peoples
    Even as a shepherd
    Foldeth his flock.

    Silent it sleeps now;
    Great ships shall seek it,
    Swarming as salmon;
    Noise of its numbers
    Two seas shall hear.

Men from the Northland,
Men from the Southland,
Haste empty-handed;
No more than manhood
Bring they, and hands.

Dark hair and fair hair,
Red blood and blue blood,
There shall be mingled;
Force of the ferment
Makes the New Man.

Pick of all kindreds,
King's blood shall theirs be,
Shoots of the eldest
Stock upon Midgard,
Sons of the poor.

Them waits the New Land;
They shall subdue it,
Leaving their sons' sons
Space for the body,
Space for the soul.

Leaving their sons' sons
All things save song-craft,
Plant long in growing,
Thrusting its tap-root
Deep in the Gone.

Here men shall grow up
Strong from self-helping;
Eyes for the present
Bring they as eagles',
Blind to the Past.

They shall make over
Creed, law, and custom;
Driving-men, doughty
Builders of empire,
Builders of men.

Here are no singers;
What should they sing of?
They, the unresting?
Labor is ugly,
Loathsome is change.

These the old gods hate,
Dwellers in dream-land,
Drinking delusion
Out of the empty
Skull of the Past.

These hate the old gods,
Warring against them;
Fatal to Odin,
Here the wolf Fenrir
Lieth in wait.

Here the gods' Twilight
Gathers, earth-gulfing;
Blackness of battle,
Fierce till the Old World
Flares up in fire.

Doubt not, my Northmen;
Fate loves the fearless;
Fools, when their roof-tree
Falls, think it doomsday;
Firm stands the sky.

Over the ruin
See I the promise;
Crisp waves the corn-field,
Peace-walled, the homestead
Waits open-doored.

There lies the New Land;
Yours to behold it,
Not to possess it;
Slowly Fate's perfect
Fulness shall come.

Then from your strong loins
Seed shall be scattered,
Men to the marrow,
Wilderness tamers,
Walkers of waves.

Jealous, the old gods
Shut it in shadow,
Wisely they ward it,
Egg of the serpent,
Bane to them all.

Stronger and sweeter
New gods shall seek it,
Fill it with man-folk
Wise for the future,
Wise from the past.

Here all is all men's,
Save only Wisdom ;
King he that wins her ;
Him hail they helmsman,
Highest of heart.

Might makes no master
Here any longer ;
Sword is not swayer ;
Here e'en the gods are
Selfish no more.

Walking the New Earth,
Lo, a divine One
Greets all men godlike,
Calls them his kindred,
He, the Divine.

Is it Thor's hammer
Rays in his right hand?
Weaponless walks he;
It is the White Christ,
Stronger than Thor.

Here shall a realm rise
Mighty in manhood;
Justice and Mercy
Here set a stronghold
Safe without spear.

Weak was the Old World,
Wearily war-fenced;
Out of its ashes,
Strong as the morning,
Springeth the New.

Beauty of promise,
Promise of beauty,
Safe in the silence
Sleep thou, till cometh
Light to thy lids!

Thee shall awaken
Flame from the furnace,
Bath of all brave ones,
Cleanser of conscience,
Kindler of will.

Lowly shall love thee,
Thee, open-handed!
Stalwart shall shield thee,
Thee, worth their best blood,
Waif of the West!

Then shall come singers,
Singing no swan-song,
Birth-carols, rather,
Meet for the man-child
Mighty of bone.

MAHMOOD THE IMAGE-BREAKER.

OLD events have modern meanings; only that survives
Of past history which finds kindred in all hearts and lives.

Mahmood once, the idol-breaker, spreader of the Faith,
Was at Sumnat tempted sorely, as the legend saith.

In the great pagoda's centre, monstrous and abhorred,
Granite on a throne of granite, sat the temple's lord.

Mahmood paused a moment, silenced by the silent face
That, with eyes of stone unwavering, awed the ancient place.

Then the Brahmins knelt before him, by his doubt
    made bold,
Pledging for their idol's ransom countless gems
    and gold.

Gold was yellow dirt to Mahmood, but of precious
    use,
Since from it the roots of power suck a potent
    juice.

"Were yon stone alone in question, this would
    please me well,"
Mahmood said; "but, with the block there, I my
    truth must sell.

"Wealth and rule slip down with Fortune, as her
    wheel turns round;
He who keeps his faith, he only cannot be dis-
    crowned.

"Little were a change of station, loss of life or
    crown,
But the wreck were past retrieving if the Man fell
    down."

So his iron mace he lifted, smote with might and main,
And the idol, on the pavement tumbling, burst in twain.

Luck obeys the downright striker; from the hollow core,
Fifty times the Brahmins' offer deluged all the floor.

INVITA MINERVA.

THE Bardling came where by a river grew
   The pennoned reeds, that, as the west-wind blew,
Gleamed and sighed plaintively, as if they knew
What music slept enchanted in each stem,
Till Pan should choose some happy one of them,
And with wise lips enlife it through and through.

The Bardling thought, "A pipe is all I need;
Once I have sought me out a clear, smooth reed,
And shaped it to my fancy, I proceed
To breathe such strains as, yonder 'mid the rocks,
The strange youth blows, that tends Admetus' flocks,
And all the maidens will to me pay heed."

The summer day he spent in questful round,
And many a reed he marred, but never found

A conjuring-spell to free the imprisoned sound;
At last his vainly wearied limbs he laid
Beneath a sacred laurel's flickering shade,
And sleep about his brain her cobweb wound.

Then strode the mighty Mother through his dreams,
Saying: "The reeds along a thousand streams
Are mine, and who is he that plots and schemes
To snare the melodies wherewith my breath
Sounds through the double pipes of Life and Death,
Atoning what to men mad discord seems?

"He seeks not me, but I seek oft in vain
For him who shall my voiceful reeds constrain,
And make them utter their melodious pain;
He flies the immortal gift, for well he knows
His life of life must with its overflows
Flood the unthankful pipe, nor come again.

"Thou fool, who dost my harmless subjects wrong,
'T is not the singer's wish that makes the song:
The rhythmic beauty wanders dumb, how long,

Nor stoops to any daintiest instrument,
Till, found its mated lips, their sweet consent
Makes mortal breath than Time and Fate more
  strong."

THE FOUNTAIN OF YOUTH.

I.

'TIS a woodland enchanted!
By no sadder spirit
Than blackbirds and thrushes,
That whistle to cheer it
All day in the bushes,
This woodland is haunted:
And in a small clearing,
Beyond sight or hearing
Of human annoyance,
The little fount gushes,
First smoothly, then dashes
And gurgles and flashes,
To the maples and ashes
Confiding its joyance;
Unconscious confiding,
Then, silent and glossy,

Slips winding and hiding.
Through alder-stems mossy,
Through gossamer roots
Fine as nerves,
That tremble, as shoots
Through their magnetized curves
The allurement delicious
Of the water's capricious
Thrills, gushes, and swerves.

II.

'T is a woodland enchanted!
I am writing no fiction;
And this fount, its sole daughter,
To the woodland was granted
To pour holy water
And win benediction;
In summer-noon flushes,
When all the wood hushes,
Blue dragon-flies knitting
To and fro in the sun,

With sidelong jerk flitting
Sink down on the rushes,
And, motionless sitting,
Hear it bubble and run,
Hear its low inward singing,
With level wings swinging
On green tasselled rushes,
To dream in the sun.

III.

'T is a woodland enchanted!
The great August noonlight,
Through myriad rifts slanted,
Leaf and bole thickly sprinkles
With flickering gold;
There, in warm August gloaming,
With quick, silent brightenings,
From meadow-lands roaming,
The firefly twinkles
His fitful heat-lightnings;
There the magical moonlight

With meek, saintly glory
Steeps summit and wold;
There whippoorwills plain in the solitudes hoary,
With lone cries that wander
Now hither, now yonder,
Like souls doomed of old
To a mild purgatory;
But through noonlight and moonlight
The little fount tinkles
Its silver saints'-bells,
That no sprite ill-boding
May make his abode in
Those innocent dells.

IV.

'T is a woodland enchanted!
When the phebe scarce whistles
Once an hour to his fellow,
And, where red lilies flaunted,
Balloons from the thistles
Tell summer's disasters,

The butterflies yellow,
As caught in an eddy
Of air's silent ocean,
Sink, waver, and steady
O'er goat's-beard and asters,
Like souls of dead flowers,
With aimless emotion
Still lingering unready
To leave their old bowers;
And the fount is no dumber,
But still gleams and flashes,
And gurgles and plashes,
To the measure of summer;
The butterflies hear it,
And spell-bound are holden,
Still balancing near it
O'er the goat's-beard so golden.

V.

'T is a woodland enchanted!
A vast silver willow,
I know not how planted,
(This wood is enchanted,
And full of surprises,)
Stands stemming a billow,
A motionless billow
Of ankle-deep mosses;
Two great roots it crosses
To make a round basin,
And there the Fount rises;
Ah, too pure a mirror
For one sick of error
To see his sad face in!
No dew-drop is stiller
In its lupin-leaf setting
Than this water moss-bounded;
But a tiny sand-pillar
From the bottom keeps jetting,

And mermaid ne'er sounded
Through the wreaths of a shell,
Down amid crimson dulses
In some dell of ocean,
A melody sweeter
Than the delicate pulses,
The soft, noiseless metre
The pause and the swell
Of that musical motion :
I recall it, not see it ;
Could vision be clearer ?
Half I'm fain to draw nearer
Half tempted to flee it ;
The sleeping Past wake not,
Beware !
One forward step take not,
Ah ! break not
That quietude rare !
By my step unaffrighted
A thrush hops before it,
And o'er it
A birch hangs delighted,

Dipping, dipping, dipping its tremulous hair;
Pure as the fountain, once
I came to the place,
(How dare I draw nearer?)
I bent o'er its mirror,
And saw a child's face
'Mid locks of bright gold in it;
Yes, pure as this fountain once, —
Since, how much error!
Too holy a mirror
For the man to behold in it
His harsh, bearded countenance!

VI.

'T is a woodland enchanted!
Ah, fly unreturning!
Yet stay; —
'T is a woodland enchanted,
Where wonderful chances
Have sway;
Luck flees from the cold one

THE FOUNTAIN OF YOUTH.

But leaps to the bold one
Half-way;
Why should I be daunted?
Still the smooth mirror glances,
Still the amber sand dances,
One look, — then away!
O magical glass!
Canst keep in thy bosom
Shades of leaf and of blossom
When summer days pass,
So that when thy wave hardens
It shapes as it pleases,
Unharmed by the breezes,
Its fine hanging gardens?
Hast those in thy keeping,
And canst not uncover,
Enchantedly sleeping,
The old shade of thy lover?
It is there! I have found it!
He wakes, the long sleeper!
The pool is grown deeper,
The sand dance is ending,

The white floor sinks, blending
With skies that below me
Are deepening and bending,
And a child's face alone
That seems not to know me,
With hair that fades golden
In the heaven-glow round it,
Looks up at my own;
Ah, glimpse through the portal
That leads to the throne,
That opes the child's olden
Regions Elysian!
Ah, too holy vision
For thy skirts to be holden
By soiled hand of mortal!
It wavers, it scatters,
'T is gone past recalling!
A tear's sudden falling
The magic cup shatters,
Breaks the spell of the waters,
And the sand cone once more,
With a ceaseless renewing,

Its dance is pursuing
On the silvery floor,
O'er and o'er,
With a noiseless and ceaseless renewing.

VII.

'Tis a woodland enchanted!
If you ask me, *Where is it?*
I only can answer,
'T is past my disclosing;
Not to choice is it granted
By sure paths to visit
The still pool enclosing
Its blithe little dancer;
But in some day, the rarest
Of many Septembers,
When the pulses of air rest,
And all things lie dreaming
In drowsy haze steaming
From the wood's glowing embers,
Then, sometimes, unheeding,

And asking not whither,
By a sweet inward leading
My feet are drawn thither,
And, looking with awe in the magical mirror,
I see through my tears,
Half doubtful of seeing,
The face unperverted,
The warm golden being
Of a child of five years;
And spite of the mists and the error,
And the days overcast,
Can feel that I walk undeserted,
But forever attended
By the glad heavens that bended
O'er the innocent past;
Toward fancy or truth
Doth the sweet vision win me?
Dare I think that I cast
In the fountain of youth
The fleeting reflection
Of some bygone perfection
That still lingers in me?

YUSSOUF.

A STRANGER came one night to Yussouf's tent,
Saying, "Behold one outcast and in dread,
Against whose life the bow of power is bent,
Who flies, and hath not where to lay his head;
I come to thee for shelter and for food,
To Yussouf, called through all our tribes "The Good."

"This tent is mine," said Yussouf, "but no more
Than it is God's; come in, and be at peace;
Freely shalt thou partake of all my store
As I of His who buildeth over these
Our tents his glorious roof of night and day,
And at whose door none ever yet heard Nay."

So Yussouf entertained his guest that night,
And, waking him ere day, said: "Here is gold,

My swiftest horse is saddled for thy flight,
Depart before the prying day grow bold."
As one lamp lights another, nor grows less,
So nobleness enkindleth nobleness.

That inward light the stranger's face made grand,
Which shines from all self-conquest; kneeling low,
He bowed his forehead upon Yussouf's hand,
Sobbing: "O Sheik, I cannot leave thee so;
I will repay thee; all this thou hast done
Unto that Ibrahim who slew thy son!"

"Take thrice the gold," said Yussouf, "for with thee
Into the desert, never to return,
My one black thought shall ride away from me;
First-born, for whom by day and night I yearn,
Balanced and just are all of God's decrees;
Thou art avenged, my first-born, sleep in peace!"

THE DARKENED MIND.

THE fire is burning clear and blithely,
  Pleasantly whistles the winter wind;
We are about thee, thy friends and kindred,
On us all flickers the firelight kind;
There thou sittest in thy wonted corner
Lone and awful in thy darkened mind.

There thou sittest; now and then thou moanest;
Thou dost talk with what we cannot see,
Lookest at us with an eye so doubtful,
It doth put us very far from thee;
There thou sittest; we would fain be nigh thee,
But we know that it can never be.

We can touch thee, still we are no nearer;
Gather round thee, still thou art alone;
The wide chasm of reason is between us;

Thou confutest kindness with a moan;
We can speak to thee, and thou canst answer,
Like two prisoners through a wall of stone.

Hardest heart would call it very awful
When thou look'st at us and seest — O what?
If we move away, thou sittest gazing
With those vague eyes at the selfsame spot,
And thou mutterest, thy hands thou wringest,
Seeing something, — us thou seëst not.

Strange it is that, in this open brightness,
Thou shouldst sit in such a narrow cell;
Strange it is that thou shouldst be so lonesome
Where those are who love thee all so well;
Not so much of thee is left among us
As the hum outliving the hushed bell.

WHAT RABBI JEHOSHA SAID.

RABBI JEHOSHA used to say
That God made angels every day,
Perfect as Michael and the rest
First brooded in creation's nest,
Whose only office was to cry
Hosanna! once, and then to die;
Or rather, with Life's essence blent,
To be led home from banishment.

Rabbi Jehosha had the skill
To know that Heaven is in God's will;
And doing that, though for a space
One heart-beat long, may win a grace
As full of grandeur and of glow
As Princes of the Chariot know.

'T were glorious, no doubt, to be
One of the strong-winged Hierarchy,

To burn with Seraphs, or to shine
With Cherubs, deathlessly divine;
Yet I, perhaps, poor earthly clod,
Could I forget myself in God,
Could I but find my nature's clew
Simply as birds and blossoms do,
And but for one rapt moment know
'T is Heaven must come, not we must go,
Should win my place as near the throne
As the pearl-angel of its zone,
And God would listen 'mid the throng
For my one breath of perfect song,
That, in its simple human way,
Said all the Host of Heaven could say.

ALL-SAINTS.

ONE feast, of holy days the crest,
   I, though no Churchman, love to keep,
All-Saints, — the unknown good that rest
   In God's still memory folded deep;
The bravely dumb that did their deed,
   And scorned to blot it with a name,
Men of the plain heroic breed,
   That loved Heaven's silence more than fame.

Such lived not in the past alone,
   But thread to-day the unheeding street,
And stairs to Sin and Famine known
   Sing with the welcome of their feet;
The den they enter grows a shrine,
   The grimy sash an oriel burns,
Their cup of water warms like wine,
   Their speech is filled from heavenly urns.

About their brows to me appears
 An aureole traced in tenderest light,
The rainbow-gleam of smiles through tears
 In dying eyes, by them made bright,
Of souls that shivered on the edge
 Of that chill ford repassed no more,
And in their mercy felt the pledge
 And sweetness of the farther shore.

A WINTER-EVENING HYMN TO MY FIRE.

I.

BEAUTY on my hearth-stone blazing!
To-night the triple Zoroaster
Shall my prophet be and master:
To-night will I pure Magian be,
Hymns to thy sole honor raising,
While thou leapest fast and faster,
Wild with self-delighted glee,
Or sink'st low and glowest faintly
As an aureole still and saintly,
Keeping cadence to my praising
Thee! still thee! and only thee!

II.

Elfish daughter of Apollo!
Thee, from thy father stolen and bound
To serve in Vulcan's clangorous smithy
Prometheus (primal Yankee) found,

And, when he had tampered with thee,
(Too confiding little maid!)
In a reed's precarious hollow
To our frozen earth conveyed:
For he swore I know not what;
Endless ease should be thy lot,
Pleasure that should never falter,
Life-long play, and not a duty
Save to hover o'er the altar,
Vision of celestial beauty,
Fed with precious woods and spices,
Then, perfidious! having got
Thee in the net of his devices,
Sold thee into endless slavery,
Made thee a drudge to boil the pot,
Thee, Helios' daughter, who dost bear
His likeness in thy golden hair;
Thee, by nature wild and wavery,
Palpitating, evanescent
As the shade of Dian's crescent,
Life, motion, gladness, everywhere!

III.

Fathom deep men bury thee
In the furnace dark and still,
There, with dreariest mockery,
Making thee eat, against thy will,
Blackest Pennsylvanian stone;
But thou dost avenge thy doom,
For, from out thy catacomb,
Day and night thy wrath is blown
In a withering simoom,
And, adown that cavern drear,
Thy black pitfall in the floor,
Staggers the lusty antique cheer,
Despairing, and is seen no more!

IV.

Elfish I may rightly name thee;
We enslave, but cannot tame thee;
With fierce snatches, now and then,
Thou pluckest at thy right again,
And thy down-trod instincts savage

To stealthy insurrection creep,
While thy wittol masters sleep,
And burst in undiscerning ravage;
Then how thou shak'st thy bacchant locks!
While brazen pulses, far and near,
Throb thick and thicker wild with fear
And dread conjecture, till the drear
Disordered clangor every steeple rocks!

v.

But when we make a friend of thee,
And admit thee to the hall
On our nights of festival,
Then, Cinderella, who could see
In thee the kitchen's stunted thrall?
Once more a Princess lithe and tall,
Thou dancest with a whispering tread,
While the bright marvel of thy head
In crinkling gold floats all abroad,
And gloriously dost vindicate
The legend of thy lineage great,
Earth-exiled daughter of the Pythian god!

Now in the ample chimney-place,
To honor thy acknowledged race,
We crown thee high with laurel good,
Thy shining father's sacred wood,
Which, guessing thy ancestral right,
Sparkles and snaps his dumb delight,
And, at thy touch, poor outcast one,
Feels through his gladdened fibres go
The tingle and thrill and vassal glow
Of instincts loyal to the sun.

VI.

O thou of home the guardian Lar,
And, when our earth hath wandered far
Into the cold, and deep snow covers
The walks of our New England lovers,
Their sweet secluded evening-star!
'T was with thy rays the English Muse
Ripened her mild domestic hues;
'T was by thy flicker that she conned
The fireside wisdom that enrings
With light from heaven familiar things;

By thee she found the homely faith
In whose mild eyes thy comfort stay'th,
When Death, extinguishing his torch,
Gropes for the latch-string in the porch;
The love that wanders not beyond
His earliest nest, but sits and sings
While children smooth his patient wings;
Therefore with thee I love to read
Our brave old poets: at thy touch how stirs
Life in the withered words! how swift recede
Time's shadows! and how glows again
Through its dead mass the incandescent verse,
As when upon the anvils of the brain
It glittering lay, cyclopically wrought
By the fast-throbbing hammers of the poet's
      thought!
Thou murmurest, too, divinely stirred,
The aspirations unattained,
The rhythms so rathe and delicate,
They bent and strained
And broke, beneath the sombre weight
Of any airiest mortal word.

VII.

What warm protection dost thou bend
Round curtained talk of friend with friend,
While the gray snow-storm, held aloof,
To softest outline rounds the roof,
Or the rude North with baffled strain
Shoulders the frost-starred window-pane!
Now the kind nymph to Bacchus borne
By Morpheus' daughter, she that seems
Gifted upon her natal morn
By him with fire, by her with dreams,
Nicotia, dearer to the Muse
Than all the grapes' bewildering juice,
We worship, unforbid of thee;
And, as her incense floats and curls
In airy spires and wayward whirls,
Or poises on its tremulous stalk
A flower of frailest revery,
So winds and loiters, idly free,
The current of unguided talk,
Now laughter-rippled, and now caught

In smooth, dark pools of deeper thought.
Meanwhile thou mellowest every word,
A sweetly unobtrusive third;
For thou hast magic beyond wine,
To unlock natures each to each;
The unspoken thought thou canst divine;
Thou fillest the pauses of the speech
With whispers that to dream-land reach,
And frozen fancy-springs unchain
In Arctic outskirts of the brain;
Sun of all inmost confidences!
To thy rays doth the heart unclose
Its formal calyx of pretences,
That close against rude day's offences,
And open its shy midnight rose.

VIII.

Thou holdest not the master key
With which thy Sire sets free the mystic gates
Of Past and Future: not for common fates
Do they wide open fling,
And, with a far-heard ring,

Swing back their willing valves melodiously;
Only to ceremonial days,
And great processions of imperial song
That set the world at gaze,
Doth such high privilege belong:
But thou a postern-door canst ope
To humbler chambers of the selfsame palace
Where Memory lodges, and her sister Hope,
Whose being is but as a crystal chalice
Which, with her various mood, the elder fills
Of joy or sorrow,
So coloring as she wills
With hues of yesterday the unconscious morrow.

IX.

Thou sinkest, and my fancy sinks with thee:
For thee I took the idle shell,
And struck the unused chords again,
But they are gone who listened well;
Some are in heaven, and all are far from me:
Even as I sing, it turns to pain,
And with vain tears my eyelids throb and swell:

Enough; I come not of the race
That hawk their sorrows in the market-place.
Earth stops the ears I best had loved to please;
Then break, ye untuned chords, or rust in peace!
As if a white-haired actor should come back
Some midnight to the theatre void and black,
And there rehearse his youth's great part
'Mid thin applauses of the ghosts,
So seems it now: ye crowd upon my heart,
And I bow down in silence, shadowy hosts!

FANCY'S CASUISTRY.

How struggles with the tempest's swells
    That warning of tumultuous bells!
The fire is loose! and frantic knells
    Throb fast and faster,
As tower to tower confusedly tells
    News of disaster.

But on my far-off solitude
No harsh alarums can intrude;
The terror comes to me subdued
    And charmed by distance,
To deepen the habitual mood
    Of my existence.

Are those, I muse, the Easter chimes?
And listen, weaving careless rhymes
While the loud city's griefs and crimes
    Pay gentle allegiance

To the fine quiet that sublimes
   These dreamy regions.

And when the storm o'erwhelms the shore,
I watch entranced as, o'er and o'er,
The light revolves amid the roar
   So still and saintly,
Now large and near, now more and more
   Withdrawing faintly.

This, too, despairing sailors see
Flash out the breakers 'neath their lee
In sudden snow, then lingeringly
   Wane tow'rd eclipse,
While through the dark the shuddering sea
   Gropes for the ships.

And is it right, this mood of mind
That thus, in revery enshrined,
Can in the world mere topics find
   For musing stricture,
Seeing the life of humankind
   Only as picture?

The events in line of battle go;
In vain for me their trumpets blow
As unto him that lieth low
    In death's dark arches,
And through the sod hears throbbing slow
    The muffled marches.

O Duty, am I dead to thee
In this my cloistered ecstasy,
In this lone shallop on the sea
    That drifts tow'rd Silence?
And are those visioned shores I see
    But sirens' islands?

My Dante frowns with lip-locked mien,
As who would say, " 'T is those, I ween,
Whom lifelong armor-chafe makes lean
    That win the laurel ";
But where *is* Truth? What does it mean,
    The world-old quarrel?

Such questionings are idle air:
Leave what to do and what to spare

To the inspiring moment's care,
    Nor ask for payment
Of fame or gold, but just to wear
    Unspotted raiment.

TO MR. JOHN BARTLETT,

WHO HAD SENT ME A SEVEN-POUND TROUT.

FIT for an Abbot of Theleme,
    For the whole Cardinals' College, or
The Pope himself to see in dream
Before his lenten vision gleam,
    He lies there, the sogdologer!

His precious flanks with stars besprent,
    Worthy to swim in Castaly!
The friend by whom such gifts are sent,
For him shall bumpers full be spent,
    His health! be Luck his fast ally!

I see him trace the wayward brook
    Amid the forest mysteries,
Where at their shades shy aspens look,
Or where, with many a gurgling crook,
    It croons its woodland histories.

I see leaf-shade and sun-fleck lend
    Their tremulous, sweet vicissitude
To smooth, dark pool, to crinkling bend, —
(O, stew him, Ann, as 't were your friend,
    With amorous solicitude !)

I see him step with caution due,
    Soft as if shod with moccasins,
Grave as in church, for who plies you,
Sweet craft, is safe as in a pew
    From all our common stock o' sins.

The unerring fly I see him cast,
    That as a rose-leaf falls as soft,
A flash ! a whirl ! he has him fast !
We tyros, how that struggle last
    Confuses and appalls us oft.

Unfluttered he : calm as the sky
    Looks on our tragi-comedies,
This way and that he lets him fly,
A sunbeam-shuttle, then to die
    Lands him, with cool *aplomb*, at ease.

The friend who gave our board such gust,
    Life's care, may he o'erstep it half,
And, when Death hooks him, as he must,
He 'll do it handsomely, I trust,
    And John H—— write his epitaph!

O, born beneath the Fishes' sign,
    Of constellations happiest,
May he somewhere with Walton dine,
May Horace send him Massic wine,
    And Burns Scotch drink, the nappiest!

And when they come his deeds to weigh,
    And how he used the talents his,
One trout-scale in the scales he 'll lay
(If trout had scales), and 't will outsway
    The wrong side of the balances.

ODE TO HAPPINESS.

SPIRIT, that rarely comest now
    And only to contrast my gloom,
Like rainbow-feathered birds that bloom
A moment on some autumn bough
That, with the spurn of their farewell,
Sheds its last leaves, — thou once didst dwell
    With me year-long, and make intense
To boyhood's wisely vacant days
Their fleet but all-sufficing grace
    Of trustful inexperience,
    While soul could still transfigure sense,
And thrill, as with love's first caress,
At life's mere unexpectedness.
    Days when my blood would leap and run
        As full of sunshine as a breeze,
        Or spray tossed up by Summer seas
    That doubts if it be sea or sun!

ODE TO HAPPINESS.

Days that flew swiftly like the band
    That played in Grecian games at strife,
And passed from eager hand to hand
    The onward-dancing torch of life!

Wing-footed! thou abid'st with him
    Who asks it not; but he who hath
    Watched o'er the waves thy waning path,
Shall nevermore behold returning
Thy high-heaped canvas shoreward yearning!
Thou first reveal'st to us thy face
Turned o'er the shoulder's parting grace,
    A moment glimpsed, then seen no more, —
Thou whose swift footsteps we can trace
    Away from every mortal door!

Nymph of the unreturning feet,
    How may I win thee back? But no,
    I do thee wrong to call thee so;
'T is I am changed, not thou art fleet:
The man thy presence feels again,
Not in the blood, but in the brain,

Spirit, that lov'st the upper air
Serene and passionless and rare,
   Such as on mountain heights we find
   And wide-viewed uplands of the mind;
Or such as scorns to coil and sing
Round any but the eagle's wing
   Of souls that with long upward beat
   Have won an undisturbed retreat
Where, poised like wingëd victories,
They mirror in relentless eyes
   The life broad-basking 'neath their feet, —
Man ever with his Now at strife,
   Pained with first gasps of earthly air,
   Then praying Death the last to spare,
Still fearful of the ampler life.

Not unto them dost thou consent
   Who, passionless, can lead at ease
A life of unalloyed content,
   A life like that of land-locked seas,
That feel no elemental gush
Of tidal forces, no fierce rush

Of storm deep-grasping scarcely spent
   'Twixt continent and continent.
Such quiet souls have never known
   Thy truer inspiration, thou
   Who lov'st to feel upon thy brow
Spray from the plunging vessel thrown
   Grazing the tusked lee shore, the cliff
That o'er the abrupt gorge holds its breath,
   Where the frail hair-breadth of an *if*
Is all that sunders life and death:
These, too, are cared-for, and round these
Bends her mild crook thy sister Peace;
   These in unvexed dependence lie,
   Each 'neath his strip of household sky;
O'er these clouds wander, and the blue
Hangs motionless the whole day through;
   Stars rise for them, and moons grow large
And lessen in such tranquil wise
As joys and sorrows do that rise
   Within their nature's sheltered marge;
Their hours into each other flit
   Like the leaf-shadows of the vine

And fig-tree under which they sit,
   And their still lives to heaven incline
With an unconscious habitude,
   Unhistoried as smokes that rise
From happy hearths and sight elude
   In kindred blue of morning skies.

Wayward! when once we feel thy lack,
'T is worse than vain to woo thee back!
   Yet there is one who seems to be
Thine elder sister, in whose eyes
A faint far northern light will rise
   Sometimes, and bring a dream of thee;
She is not that for which youth hoped,
   But she hath blessings all her own,
Thoughts pure as lilies newly oped,
   And faith to sorrow given alone;
Almost I deem that it is thou
Come back with graver matron brow,
   With deepened eyes and bated breath,
   Like one that somewhere hath met Death.
But "No," she answers, "I am she

Whom the gods love, Tranquillity;
  That other whom you seek forlorn
  Half earthly was; but I am born
Of the immortals, and our race
Wear still some sadness on our face:
  He wins me late, but keeps me long,
Who, dowered with every gift of passion,
In that fierce flame can forge and fashion
  Of sin and self the anchor strong;
Can thence compel the driving force
Of daily life's mechanic course,
Nor less the nobler energies
Of needful toil and culture wise;
Whose soul is worth the tempter's lure
Who can renounce, and yet endure,
To him I come, not lightly wooed,
But won by silent fortitude."

VILLA FRANCA.

1859.

WAIT a little: do *we* not wait?
　　Louis Napoleon is not Fate,
Francis Joseph is not Time;
There 's One hath swifter feet than Crime;
Cannon-parliaments settle naught;
Venice is Austria's, — whose is Thought?
Minié is good, but, spite of change,
Gutenberg's gun has the longest range.
　　Spin, spin, Clotho, spin!
　　Lachesis, twist! and Atropos, sever!
　　In the shadow, year out, year in,
　　The silent headsman waits forever.

Wait, we say: our years are long;
Men are weak, but Man is strong;
Since the stars first curved their rings,
We have looked on many things;

Great wars come and great wars go,
Wolf-tracks light on polar snow;
We shall see him come and gone,
This second-hand Napoleon.
    Spin, spin, Clotho, spin!
    Lachesis, twist! and Atropos, sever!
    In the shadow, year out, year in,
    The silent headsman waits forever.

We saw the elder Corsican,
And Clotho muttered as she span,
While crowned lackeys bore the train,
Of the pinchbeck Charlemagne:
"Sister, stint not length of thread!
Sister, stay the scissors dread!
On Saint Helen's granite bleak,
Hark, the vulture whets his beak!"
    Spin, spin, Clotho, spin!
    Lachesis, twist! and Atropos, sever!
    In the shadow, year out, year in,
    The silent headsman waits forever.

The Bonapartes, we know their bees
That wade in honey red to the knees;
Their patent reaper, its sheaves sleep sound
In dreamless garners underground;
We know false glory's spendthrift race
Pawning nations for feathers and lace;
It may be short, it may be long,
"'T is reckoning-day!" sneers unpaid Wrong.
    Spin, spin, Clotho, spin!
    Lachesis, twist! and Atropos, sever!
    In the shadow, year out, year in,
    The silent headsman waits forever.

The Cock that wears the Eagle's skin
Can promise what he ne'er could win;
Slavery reaped for fine words sown,
System for all, and rights for none,
Despots atop, a wild clan below,
Such is the Gaul from long ago;
Wash the black from the Ethiop's face,
Wash the past out of man or race!

VILLA FRANCA.

    Spin, spin, Clotho, spin!
    Lachesis, twist! and Atropos, sever!
    In the shadow, year out, year in,
    The silent headsman waits forever.

'Neath Gregory's throne a spider swings,
And snares the people for the kings;
"Luther is dead; old quarrels pass;
The stake's black scars are healed with grass";
So dreamers prate; did man e'er live
Saw priest or woman yet forgive?
But Luther's broom is left, and eyes
Peep o'er their creeds to where it lies.
    Spin, spin, Clotho, spin!
    Lachesis, twist! and Atropos, sever!
    In the shadow, year out, year in,
    The silent headsman waits forever.

Smooth sails the ship of either realm,
Kaiser and Jesuit at the helm;
We look down the depths, and mark
Silent workers in the dark

Building slow the sharp-tusked reefs,
Old instincts hardening to new beliefs;
Patience a little; learn to wait;
Hours are long on the clock of Fate.
  Spin, spin, Clotho, spin!
  Lachesis, twist! and Atropos, sever!
  Darkness is strong, and so is Sin,
  But only God endures forever!

THE MINER.

DOWN 'mid the tangled roots of things
    That coil about the central fire,
I seek for that which giveth wings
    To stoop, not soar, to my desire.

Sometimes I hear, as 't were a sigh,
    The sea's deep yearning far above,
"Thou hast the secret not," I cry,
    "In deeper deeps is hid my Love."

They think I burrow from the sun,
    In darkness, all alone, and weak;
Such loss were gain if He were won,
    For 't is the sun's own Sun I seek.

"The earth," they murmur, "is the tomb
    That vainly sought his life to prison;

Why grovel longer in the gloom?
    He is not here; he hath arisen."

More life for me where he hath lain
    Hidden while ye believed him dead,
Than in cathedrals cold and vain,
    Built on loose sands of *It is said*.

My search is for the living gold;
    Him I desire who dwells recluse,
And not his image worn and old,
    Day-servant of our sordid use.

If him I find not, yet I find
    The ancient joy of cell and church,
The glimpse, the surety undefined,
    The unquenched ardor of the search.

Happier to chase a flying goal
    Than to sit counting laurelled gains,
To guess the Soul within the soul
    Than to be lord of what remains.

Hide still, best Good, in subtile wise,
  Beyond my nature's utmost scope;
Be ever absent from mine eyes
  To be twice present in my hope!

GOLD EGG: A DREAM-FANTASY.

HOW A STUDENT IN SEARCH OF THE BEAUTIFUL, FELL ASLEEP IN DRESDEN OVER HERR PROFESSOR DOCTOR VISCHER'S WISSENSCHAFT DES SCHÖNEN, AND WHAT CAME THEREOF.

I SWAM with undulation soft,
   Adrift on Vischer's ocean,
And, from my cockboat up aloft,
Sent down my mental plummet oft
   In hope to reach a notion.

But from the metaphysic sea
   No bottom was forthcoming,
And all the while (how drearily!)
In one eternal note of B
   My German stove kept humming.

"What's Beauty?" mused I; "is it told
   By synthesis? analysis?

·Have you not made us lead of gold?
To feed your crucible, not sold
   Our temple's sacred chalices?"

Then o'er my senses came a change;
   My book seemed all traditions,
Old legends of profoundest range,
Diablery, and stories strange
   Of goblins, elves, magicians.

Old gods in modern saints I found,
   Old creeds in strange disguises;
I thought them safely underground,
And here they were, all safe and sound,
   Without a sign of phthisis.

Truth was, my outward eyes were closed,
   Although I did not know it;
Deep into dream-land I had dozed,
And so was happily transposed
   From proser into poet.

So what I read took flesh and blood,
   And turned to living creatures;
The words were but the dingy bud
That bloomed, like Adam, from the mud,
   To human forms and features.

I saw how Zeus was lodged once more
   By Baucis and Philemon;
The text said, "Not alone of yore,
But every day, at every door,
   Knocks still the masking Demon."

DAIMON 't was printed in the book,
   And, as I read it slowly,
The letters stirred and changed, and took
Jove's stature, the Olympian look
   Of painless melancholy.

He paused upon the threshold worn:
   "With coin I cannot pay you;
Yet would I fain make some return;
The gift for cheapness do not spurn,
   Accept this hen, I pray you.

"Plain feathers wears my Hemera,
   And has from ages olden;
She makes her nest in common hay,
And yet, of all the birds that lay,
   Her eggs alone are golden."

He turned, and could no more be seen;
   Old Baucis stared a moment,
Then tossed poor Partlet on the green,
And with a tone, half jest, half spleen,
   Thus made her housewife's comment:

"The stranger had a queerish face,
   His smile was hardly pleasant,
And, though he meant it for a grace,
Yet this old hen of barnyard race
   Was but a stingy present.

"She's quite too old for laying eggs,
   Nay, even to make a soup of;
One only needs to see her legs, —
You might as well boil down the pegs
   I made the brood-hen's coop of!

"Some eighteen score of such do I
    Raise every year, her sisters;
Go, in the woods your fortunes try,
All day for one poor earthworm pry,
    And scratch your toes to blisters!"

Philemon found the rede was good,
    And, turning on the poor hen,
He clapt his hands, and stamped, and shooed,
Hunting the exile tow'rd the wood,
    To house with snipe and moor-hen.

A poet saw and cried: "Hold! hold!
    What are you doing, madman?
Spurn you more wealth than can be told,
The fowl that lays the eggs of gold,
    Because she's plainly clad, man?"

To him Philemon: "I'll not balk
    Thy will with any shackle;
Wilt add a burden to thy walk?
There! take her without further talk;
    You're both but fit to cackle!"

But scarce the poet touched the bird,
   It swelled to stature regal;
And when her cloud-wide wings she stirred,
A whisper as of doom was heard,
   'T was Jove's bolt-bearing eagle.

As when from far-off cloud-bergs springs
   A crag, and, hurtling under,
From cliff to cliff the rumor flings,
So she from flight-foreboding wings
   Shook out a murmurous thunder.

She gripped the poet to her breast,
   And, ever upward soaring,
Earth seemed a new moon in the west,
And then one light among the rest
   Where squadrons lie at mooring.

How tell to what heaven-hallowed seat
   The eagle bent his courses?
The waves that on its bases beat,
The gales that round it weave and fleet,
   Are life's creative forces.

Here was the bird's primeval nest,
  High on a promontory
Star-pharosed, where she takes her rest
To brood new æons 'neath her breast,
  The future's unfledged glory.

I know not how, but I was there
  All feeling, hearing, seeing;
It was not wind that stirred my hair
But living breath, the essence rare
  Of unembodied being.

And in the nest an egg of gold
  Lay soft in self-made lustre;
Gazing whereon, what depths untold
Within, what marvels manifold,
  Seemed silently to muster!

Daily such splendors to confront
  Is still to me and you sent?
It glowed as when Saint Peter's front,
Illumed, forgets its stony wont,
  And seems to throb translucent.

One saw therein the life of man,
   (Or so the poet found it,)
The yolk and white, conceive who can,
Were the glad earth, that, floating, span
   In the glad heaven around it.

I knew this as one knows in dream,
   Where no effects to causes
Are chained as in our work-day scheme,
And then was wakened by a scream
   That seemed to come from Baucis.

"Bless Zeus!" she cried, "I'm safe below!"
   First pale, then red as coral;
And I, still drowsy, pondered slow,
And seemed to find, but hardly know,
   Something like this for moral.

Each day the world is born anew
   For him who takes it rightly;
Not fresher that which Adam knew,
Not sweeter that whose moonlit dew
   Entranced Arcadia nightly.

Rightly? That's simply: 't is to see
   Some substance casts these shadows
Which we call Life and History,
That aimless seem to chase and flee
   Like wind-gleams over meadows.

Simply? That's nobly: 't is to know
   That God may still be met with,
Nor groweth old, nor doth bestow
These senses fine, this brain aglow,
   To grovel and forget with.

Beauty, Herr Doctor, trust in me,
   No chemistry will win you;
Charis still rises from the sea;
If you can't find her, *might* it be
   Because you seek within you?

A FAMILIAR EPISTLE TO A FRIEND.

ALIKE I hate to be your debtor,
Or write a mere perfunctory letter;
For letters, so it seems to me,
Our careless quintessence should be,
Our real nature's truant play
When Consciousness looks t' other way,
Not drop by drop, with watchful skill,
Gathered in Art's deliberate still,
But life's insensible completeness
Got as the ripe grape gets its sweetness,
As if it had a way to fuse
The golden sunlight into juice.
Hopeless my mental pump I try;
The boxes hiss, the tube is dry;
As those petroleum wells that spout
Awhile like M. C.'s, then give out,
My spring, once full as Arethusa,

Is a mere bore as dry 's Creusa;
And yet you ask me why I 'm glum,
And why my graver Muse is dumb.
Ah me! I 've reasons manifold
Condensed in one, — I 'm getting old!

When life, once past its fortieth year,
Wheels up its evening hemisphere,
The mind's own shadow, which the boy
Saw onward point to hope and joy,
Shifts round, irrevocably set
Tow'rd morning's loss and vain regret,
And, argue with it as we will,
The clock is unconverted still.

"But count the gains," I hear you say,
"Which far the seeming loss outweigh;
Friendships built firm 'gainst flood and wind
On rock-foundations of the mind;
Knowledge instead of scheming hope;
For wild adventure, settled scope;
Talents, from surface-ore profuse,

Tempered and edged to tools for use;
Judgment, for passion's headlong whirls;
Old sorrows crystalled into pearls;
Losses by patience turned to gains,
Possessions now, that once were pains;
Joy's blossom gone, as go it must,
To ripen seeds of faith and trust;
Why heed a snow-flake on the roof
If fire within keep Age aloof,
Though blundering north-winds push and strain
With palms benumbed against the pane?"

My dear old Friend, you're very wise;
We always are with others' eyes,
And see *so* clear! (our neighbor's deck on)
What reef the idiot's sure to wreck on;
Folks when they learn how life has quizzed 'em
Are fain to make a shift with Wisdom,
And, finding she nor breaks nor bends,
Give her a letter to their friends.
Draw passion's torrent whoso will
Through sluices smooth to turn a mill,

And, taking solid toll of grist,
Forget the rainbow in the mist,
The exulting leap, the aimless haste
Scattered in iridescent waste ;
Prefer who likes the sure esteem
To cheated youth's midsummer dream,
When every friend was more than Damon,
Each quicksand safe to build a fame on ;
Believe that prudence snug excels
Youth's gross of verdant spectacles,
Through which earth's withered stubble seen
Looks autumn-proof as painted green, —
I side with Moses 'gainst the masses,
Take you the drudge, give me the glasses!
And, for your talents shaped with practice,
Convince me first that such the fact is ;
Let whoso likes be beat, poor fool,
On life's hard stithy to a tool,
Be whoso will a ploughshare made,
Let me remain a jolly blade!

What 's Knowledge, with her stocks and lands,
To gay Conjecture's yellow strands ?

What's watching her slow flock's increase
To ventures for the golden fleece?
What her deep ships, safe under lee,
To youth's light craft, that drinks the sea,
For Flying Islands making sail,
And failing where 't is gain to fail?
Ah me! Experience (so we 're told),
Time's crucible, turns lead to gold;
Yet what 's experience won but dross,
Cloud-gold transmuted to our loss?
What but base coin the best event
To the untried experiment?

'T was an old couple, says the poet,
That lodged the gods and did not know it;
Youth sees and knows them as they were
Before Olympus' top was bare;
From Swampscot's flats his eye divine
Sees Venus rocking on the brine,
With lucent limbs, that somehow scatter a
Charm that turns Doll to Cleopatra;
Bacchus (that now is scarce induced

To give Eld's lagging blood a boost),
With cymbals' clang and pards to draw him,
Divine as Ariadne saw him,
Storms through Youth's pulse with all his train,
And wins new Indies in his brain;
Apollo (with the old a trope,
A sort of finer Mister Pope),
Apollo —— but the Muse forbids;
At his approach cast down thy lids,
And think it joy enough to hear
Far off his arrows singing clear;
He knows enough who silent knows
The quiver chiming as he goes;
He tells too much who e'er betrays
The shining Archer's secret ways.

Dear Friend, you 're right and I am wrong;
My quibbles are not worth a song,
And I sophistically tease
My fancy sad to tricks like these.
I could not cheat you if I would;
You know me and my jesting mood,

Mere surface-foam, for pride concealing
The purpose of my deeper feeling.
I have not spilt one drop of joy
Poured in the senses of the boy,
Nor Nature fails my walks to bless
With all her golden inwardness;
And as blind nestlings, unafraid,
Stretch up wide-mouthed to every shade
By which their downy dream is stirred,
Taking it for the mother-bird;
So, when God's shadow, which is light,
Unheralded, by day or night,
My wakening instincts falls across,
Silent as sunbeams over moss,
In my heart's nest half-conscious things
Stir with a helpless sense of wings,
Lift themselves up, and tremble long
With premonitions sweet of song.

Be patient, and perhaps (who knows?)
These may be winged one day like those;
If thrushes, close-embowered to sing,

Pierced through with June's delicious sting;
If swallows, their half-hour to run
Star-breasted in the setting sun.
At first they're but the unfledged proem,
Or songless schedule of a poem;
When from the shell they're hardly dry
If some folks thrust them forth, must I?

But let me end with a comparison
Never yet hit upon by e'er a son
Of our American Apollo,
(And there's where I shall beat them hollow,
If he is not a courtly St. John,
But, as West said, a Mohawk Injun.)
A poem's like a cruise for whales:
Through untried seas the hunter sails,
His prow dividing waters known
To the blue iceberg's hulk alone;
At last, on farthest edge of day,
He marks the smoky puff of spray;
Then with bent oars the shallop flies
To where the basking quarry lies;

Then the excitement of the strife,
The crimsoned waves, — ah, this is life!

But, the dead plunder once secured
And safe beside the vessel moored,
All that had stirred the blood before
Is so much blubber, nothing more,
(I mean no pun, nor image so
Mere sentimental verse, you know,)
And all is tedium, smoke, and soil,
In trying-out the noisome oil.

Yes, this *is* life! And so the bard
Through briny deserts, never scarred
Since Noah's keel, a subject seeks,
And lies upon the watch for weeks;
That once harpooned and helpless lying,
What follows is but weary trying.

Now I've a notion, if a poet
Beat up for themes, his verse will show it;
I wait for subjects that hunt me,

By day or night won't let me be,
And hang about me like a curse,
Till they have made me into verse,
From line to line my fingers tease
Beyond my knowledge, as the bees
Build no new cell till those before
With limpid summer-sweet run o'er;
Then, if I neither sing nor shine,
Is it the subject's fault, or mine?

AN EMBER PICTURE.

How strange are the freaks of memory!
   The lessons of life we forget,
While a trifle, a trick of color,
   In the wonderful web is set,—

Set by some mordant of fancy,
   And, spite of the wear and tear
Of time or distance or trouble,
   Insists on its right to be there.

A chance had brought us together;
   Our talk was of matters-of-course;
We were nothing, one to the other,
   But a short half-hour's resource.

We spoke of French acting and actors,
   And their easy, natural way;

Of the weather, for it was raining
    As we drove home from the play.

We debated the social nothings
    We bore ourselves so to discuss;
The thunderous rumors of battle
    Were silent the while for us.

Arrived at her door, we left her
    With a drippingly hurried adieu,
And our wheels went crunching the gravel
    Of the oak-darkened avenue.

As we drove away through the shadow,
    The candle she held in the door
From rain-varnished tree-trunk to tree-trunk
    Flashed fainter, and flashed no more;—

Flashed fainter, then wholly faded
    Before we had passed the wood;
But the light of the face behind it
    Went with me and stayed for good.

AN EMBER PICTURE.

The vision of scarce a moment,
   And hardly marked at the time,
It comes unbidden to haunt me,
   Like a scrap of ballad-rhyme.

Had she beauty? Well, not what they call so;
   You may find a thousand as fair;
And yet there's her face in my memory
   With no special claim to be there.

As I sit sometimes in the twilight,
   And call back to life in the coals
Old faces and hopes and fancies
   Long buried, (good rest to their souls!)

Her face shines out in the embers;
   I see her holding the light,
And hear the crunch of the gravel
   And the sweep of the rain that night.

'T is a face that can never grow older,
   That never can part with its gleam,
'T is a gracious possession forever,
   For is it not all a dream?

TO H. W. L.,

ON HIS BIRTHDAY, 27TH FEBRUARY, 1867.

I NEED not praise the sweetness of his song,
   Where limpid verse to limpid verse succeeds
Smooth as our Charles, when, fearing lest he wrong
   The new moon's mirrored skiff, he slides along,
   Full without noise, and whispers in his reeds.

With loving breath of all the winds his name
   Is blown about the world, but to his friends
A sweeter secret hides behind his fame,
And Love steals shyly through the loud acclaim
   To murmur a *God bless you!* and there ends.

As I muse backward up the checkered years
   Wherein so much was given, so much was lost,
Blessings in both kinds, such as cheapen tears,—
But hush! this is not for profaner ears;
   Let them drink molten pearls nor dream the cost.

Some suck up poison from a sorrow's core,
   As naught but nightshade grew upon earth's ground;
Love turned all his to heart's-ease, and the more
Fate tried his bastions, she but forced a door
   Leading to sweeter manhood and more sound.

Even as a wind-waved fountain's swaying shade
   Seems of mixed race, a gray wraith shot with sun,
So through his trial faith translucent rayed
Till darkness, half disnatured so, betrayed
   A heart of sunshine that would fain o'errun.

Surely if skill in song the shears may stay
   And of its purpose cheat the charmed abyss,
If our poor life be lengthened by a lay,
He shall not go, although his presence may,
   And the next age in praise shall double this.

Long days be his, and each as lusty-sweet
   As gracious natures find his song to be;
May Age steal on with softly-cadenced feet
Falling in music, as for him were meet
   Whose choicest verse is harsher-toned than he!

THE NIGHTINGALE IN THE STUDY.

"COME forth!" my catbird calls to me,
    "And hear me sing a cavatina
That, in this old familiar tree,
    Shall hang a garden of Alcina.

"These buttercups shall brim with wine
    Beyond all Lesbian juice or Massic;
May not New England be divine?
    My ode to ripening summer classic?

"Or, if to me you will not hark,
    By Beaver Brook a thrush is ringing
Till all the alder-coverts dark
    Seem sunshine-dappled with his singing.

"Come out beneath the unmastered sky,
    With its emancipating spaces,

And learn to sing as well as I,
   Without premeditated graces.

"What boot your many-volumed gains,
   Those withered leaves forever turning,
To win, at best, for all your pains,
   A nature mummy-wrapt in learning?

"The leaves wherein true wisdom lies
   On living trees the sun are drinking;
Those white clouds, drowsing through the skies,
   Grew not so beautiful by thinking.

"Come out! with me the oriole cries,
   Escape the demon that pursues you!
And, hark, the cuckoo weatherwise,
   Still hiding, farther onward wooes you."

"Alas, dear friend, that, all my days,
   Hast poured from that syringa thicket
The quaintly discontinuous lays
   To which I hold a season-ticket,

"A season-ticket cheaply bought
　　With a dessert of pilfered berries,
And who so oft my soul hast caught
　　With morn and evening voluntaries,

"Deem me not faithless, if all day
　　Among my dusty books I linger,
No pipe, like thee, for June to play
　　With fancy-led, half-conscious finger.

"A bird is singing in my brain
　　And bubbling o'er with mingled fancies,
Gay, tragic, rapt, right heart of Spain
　　Fed with the sap of old romances.

"I ask no ampler skies than those
　　His magic music rears above me,
No falser friends, no truer foes, —
　　And does not Doña Clara love me?

"Cloaked shapes, a twanging of guitars,
　　A rush of feet, and rapiers clashing,

Then silence deep with breathless stars,
    And overhead a white hand flashing.

"O music of all moods and climes,
    Vengeful, forgiving, sensuous, saintly,
Where still, between the Christian chimes,
    The Moorish cymbal tinkles faintly!

"O life borne lightly in the hand,
    For friend or foe with grace Castilian!
O valley safe in Fancy's land,
    Not tramped to mud yet by the million!

"Bird of to-day, thy songs are stale
    To his, my singer of all weathers,.
My Calderon, my nightingale,
    My Arab soul in Spanish feathers.

"Ah, friend, these singers dead so long,
    And still, God knows, in purgatory,
Give its best sweetness to all song,
    To Nature's self her better glory."

IN THE TWILIGHT.

MEN say the sullen instrument,
    That, from the Master's bow,
  With pangs of joy or woe,
Feels music's soul through every fibre sent,
  Whispers the ravished strings
More than he knew or meant;
  Old summers in its memory glow;
  The secrets of the wind it sings;
  It hears the April-loosened springs;
    And mixes with its mood
    All it dreamed when it stood
    In the murmurous pine-wood
      Long ago!

  The magical moonlight then
    Steeped every bough and cone;
  The roar of the brook in the glen
    Came dim from the distance blown;

IN THE TWILIGHT.

The wind through its glooms sang low,
  And it swayed to and fro
    With delight as it stood,
  In the wonderful wood,
      Long ago!

O my life, have we not had seasons
  That only said, Live and rejoice?
That asked not for causes and reasons,
  But made us all feeling and voice?
When we went with the winds in their blowing,
  When Nature and we were peers,
And we seemed to share in the flowing
  Of the inexhaustible years?
  Have we not from the earth drawn juices
  Too fine for earth's sordid uses?
    Have I heard, have I seen
      All I feel and I know?
    Doth my heart overween?
    Or could it have been
        Long ago?

Sometimes a breath floats by me,
   An odor from Dreamland sent,
That makes the ghost seem nigh me
   Of a splendor that came and went,
Of a life lived somewhere, I know not
   In what diviner sphere,
Of memories that stay not and go not,
   Like music heard once by an ear
     That cannot forget or reclaim it,
      A something so shy, it would shame it
        To make it a show,
      A something too vague, could I name it,
        For others to know,
     As if I had lived it or dreamed it,
     As if I had acted or schemed it,
       Long ago!

And yet, could I live it over,
   This life that stirs in my brain,
Could I be both maiden and lover,
Moon and tide, bee and clover,
   As I seem to have been, once again,

Could I but speak and show it,
  This pleasure more sharp than pain,
    That baffles and lures me so,
The world should not lack a poet,
  Such as it had
  In the ages glad,
    Long ago!

THE FOOT-PATH.

IT mounts athwart the windy hill
   Through sallow slopes of upland bare,
And Fancy climbs with foot-fall still
   Its narrowing curves that end in air.

By day, a warmer-hearted blue
   Stoops softly to that topmost swell;
Thy thread-like windings seem a clew
   To gracious climes where all is well.

By night, far yonder, I surmise
   An ampler world than clips my ken,
Where the great stars of happier skies
   Commingle nobler fates of men.

I look and long, then haste me home,
   Still master of my secret rare;

Once tried, the path would end in Rome,
  But now it leads me everywhere.

Forever to the new it guides,
  From former good, old overmuch;
What Nature for her poets hides,
  'T is wiser to divine than clutch.

The bird I list hath never come
  Within the scope of mortal ear;
My prying step would make him dumb,
  And the fair tree, his shelter, scar.

Behind the hill, behind the sky,
  Behind my inmost thought, he sings;
No feet avail; to hear it nigh,
  The song itself must lend the wings.

Sing on, sweet bird, close hid, and raise
  Those angel stairways in my brain,
That climb from these low-vaulted days
  To spacious sunshines far from pain.

Sing when thou wilt, enchantment fleet,
  I leave thy covert haunt untrod,
And envy Science not her feat
  To make a twice-told tale of God.

They said the fairies tript no more,
  And long ago that Pan was dead;
'T was but that fools preferred to bore
  Earth's rind inch-deep for truth instead.

Pan leaps and pipes all summer long,
  The fairies dance each full-mooned night,
Would we but doff our lenses strong,
  And trust our wiser eyes' delight.

City of Elf-land, just without
  Our seeing, marvel ever new,
Glimpsed in fair weather, a sweet doubt
  Sketched-in, mirage-like, on the blue.

I build thee in yon sunset cloud,
  Whose edge allures to climb the height;

I hear thy drowned bells, inly-loud,
    From still pools dusk with dreams of night.

Thy gates are shut to hardiest will,
    Thy countersign of long-lost speech, —
Those fountained courts, those chambers still,
    Fronting Time's far East, who shall reach?

I know not and will never pry,
    But trust our human heart for all;
Wonders that from the seeker fly,
    Into an open sense may fall.

Hide in thine own soul, and surprise
    The password of the unwary elves;
Seek it, thou canst not bribe their spies;
    Unsought, they whisper it themselves.

POEMS OF THE WAR.

THE WASHERS OF THE SHROUD.

October, 1861.

ALONG a river-side, I know not where,
   I walked one night in mystery of dream;
A chill creeps curdling yet beneath my hair,
To think what chanced me by the pallid gleam
Of a moon-wraith that waned through haunted air.

Pale fireflies pulsed within the meadow-mist
Their halos, wavering thistledowns of light;
The loon, that seemed to mock some goblin tryst,
Laughed; and the echoes, huddling in affright,
Like Odin's hounds, fled baying down the night.

Then all was silent, till there smote my ear
A movement in the stream that checked my breath:
Was it the slow plash of a wading deer?

But something said, "This water is of Death!
The Sisters wash a shroud,—ill thing to hear!"

I, looking then, beheld the ancient Three
Known to the Greek's and to the Northman's creed,
That sit in shadow of the mystic Tree,
Still crooning, as they weave their endless brede,
One song: "Time was, Time is, and Time shall
    be."

No wrinkled crones were they, as I had deemed,
But fair as yesterday, to-day, to-morrow,
To mourner, lover, poet, ever seemed;
Something too high for joy, too deep for sorrow,
Thrilled in their tones, and from their faces gleamed.

"Still men and nations reap as they have strawn,"
So sang they, working at their task the while;
"The fatal raiment must be cleansed ere dawn:
For Austria? Italy? the Sea-Queen's isle?
O'er what quenched grandeur must our shroud be
    drawn?

"Or is it for a younger, fairer corse,
That gathered States for children round his knees,
That tamed the wave to be his posting-horse,
Feller of forests, linker of the seas,
Bridge-builder, hammerer, youngest son of Thor's?

"What make we, murmur'st thou? and what are we?
When empires must be wound, we bring the shroud,
The time-old web of the implacable Three:
Is it too coarse for him, the young and proud?
Earth's mightiest deigned to wear it, — why not
    he?"

"Is there no hope?" I moaned, "so strong, so
    fair!
Our Fowler whose proud bird would brook erewhile
No rival's swoop in all our western air!
Gather the ravens, then, in funeral file
For him, life's morn yet golden in his hair?

"Leave me not hopeless, ye unpitying dames!
I see, half seeing. Tell me, ye who scanned
The stars, Earth's elders, still must noblest aims

Be traced upon oblivious ocean-sands?
Must Hesper join the wailing ghosts of names?"

"When grass-blades stiffen with red battle-dew,
Ye deem we choose the victor and the slain:
Say, choose we them that shall be leal and true
To the heart's longing, the high faith of brain?
Yet there the victory lies, if ye but knew.

"Three roots bear up Dominion: Knowledge, Will, —
These twain are strong, but stronger yet the third, —
Obedience, — 't is the great tap-root that still,
Knit round the rock of Duty, is not stirred,
Though Heaven-loosed tempests spend their utmost skill.

"Is the doom sealed for Hesper? 'T is not we
Denounce it, but the Law before all time:
The brave makes danger opportunity;
The waverer, paltering with the chance sublime,
Dwarfs it to peril: which shall Hesper be?

"Hath he let vultures climb his eagle's seat
To make Jove's bolts purveyors of their maw?
Hath he the Many's plaudits found more sweet
Than Wisdom? held Opinion's wind for Law?
Then let him hearken for the doomster's feet!

"Rough are the steps, slow-hewn in flintiest rock,
States climb to power by; slippery those with gold
Down which they stumble to eternal mock:
No chafferer's hand shall long the sceptre hold,
Who, given a Fate to shape, would sell the block.

"We sing old Sagas, songs of weal and woe,
Mystic because too cheaply understood;
Dark sayings are not ours; men hear and know,
See Evil weak, see strength alone in Good,
Yet hope to stem God's fire with walls of tow.

"Time Was unlocks the riddle of Time Is,
That offers choice of glory or of gloom;
The solver makes Time Shall Be surely his.

But hasten, Sisters! for even now the tomb
Grates its slow hinge and calls from the abyss."

"But not for him," I cried, "not yet for him,
Whose large horizon, westering, star by star
Wins from the void to where on Ocean's rim
The sunset shuts the world with golden bar,
Not yet his thews shall fail, his eye grow dim!

"His shall be larger manhood, saved for those
That walk unblenching through the trial-fires;
Not suffering, but faint heart, is worst of woes,
And he no base-born son of craven sires,
Whose eye need blench confronted with his foes.

"Tears may be ours, but proud, for those who win
Death's royal purple in the foeman's lines;
Peace, too, brings tears; and 'mid the battle-din,
The wiser ear some text of God divines,
For the sheathed blade may rust with darker sin.

"God, give us peace! not such as lulls to sleep,
But sword on thigh, and brow with purpose knit!
And let our Ship of State to harbor sweep,
Her ports all up, her battle-lanterns lit,
And her leashed thunders gathering for their leap!"

So cried I with clenched hands and passionate pain,
Thinking of dear ones by Potomac's side;
Again the loon laughed mocking, and again
The echoes bayed far down the night and died,
While waking I recalled my wandering brain.

TWO SCENES FROM THE LIFE OF BLONDEL.

Autumn, 1863.

Scene I. — *Near a Castle in Germany.*

'T WERE no hard task, perchance, to win
   The popular laurel for my song;
'T were only to comply with sin,
   And own the crown, though snatched by wrong:
Rather Truth's chaplet let me wear,
   Though sharp as death its thorns may sting;
Loyal to Loyalty, I bear
   No badge but of my rightful king.

Patient by town and tower I wait,
   Or o'er the blustering moorland go;
I buy no praise at cheaper rate,
   Or what faint hearts may fancy so;
For me, no joy in lady's bower,
   Or hall, or tourney, will I sing,

Till the slow stars wheel round the hour
    That crowns my hero and my king.

While all the land runs red with strife,
    And wealth is won by pedler-crimes,
Let who will find content in life
    And tinkle in unmanly rhymes;
I wait and seek; through dark and light,
    Safe in my heart my hope I bring,
Till I once more my faith may plight
    To him my whole soul owns her king.

When power is filched by drone and dolt,
    And, with caught breath and flashing eye,
Her knuckles whitening round the bolt,
    Vengeance leans eager from the sky,
While this and that the people guess,
    And to the skirts of praters cling,
Who court the crowd they should compress,
    I turn in scorn to seek my king.

Shut in what tower of darkling chance
    Or dungeon of a narrow doom,
Dream'st thou of battle-axe and lance
    That for the Cross make crashing room?
Come! with hushed breath the battle waits
    In the wild van thy mace's swing;
While doubters parley with their fates,
    Make thou thine own and ours, my king!

O, strong to keep upright the old,
    And wise to buttress with the new,
Prudent, as only are the bold,
    Clear-eyed, as only are the true,
To foes benign, to friendship stern,
    Intent to imp Law's broken wing,
Who would not die, if death might earn
    The right to kiss thy hand, my king?

Scene II. — *An Inn near the Château of Chalus.*

WELL, the whole thing is over, and here I sit
   With one arm in a sling and a milk-score of gashes,
And this flagon of Cyprus must e'en warm my wit,
   Since what's left of youth's flame is a head flecked with ashes.
I remember I sat in this very same inn, —
   I was young then, and one young man thought I was handsome, —
I had found out what prison King Richard was in,
   And was spurring for England to push on the ransom.

How I scorned the dull souls that sat guzzling around
   And knew not my secret nor recked my derision!
Let the world sink or swim, John or Richard be crowned,
   All one, so the beer-tax got lenient revision.

How little I dreamed, as I tramped up and down,
  That granting our wish one of Fate's saddest
      jokes is!
I had mine with a vengeance, — my king got his
      crown,
  And made his whole business to break other
      folks's.

I might as well join in the safe old *tum, tum:*
  A hero's an excellent loadstar, — but, bless ye,
What infinite odds 'twixt a hero to come
  And your only too palpable hero *in esse!*
Precisely the odds (such examples are rife)
  'Twixt the poem conceived and the rhyme we
      make show of,
'Twixt the boy's morning dream and the wake-up
      of life,
  'Twixt the Blondel God meant and a Blondel I
      know of!

But the world's better off, I'm convinced of it now,
  Than if heroes, like buns, could be bought for a
      penny

To regard all mankind as their haltered milch-cow,
  And just care for themselves. Well, God cares
    for the many;
For somehow the poor old Earth blunders along,
  Each son of hers adding his mite of unfitness,
And, choosing the sure way of coming out wrong,
  Gets to port, as the next generation will witness.

You think her old ribs have come all crashing
    through,
  If a whisk of Fate's broom snap your cobweb
    asunder;
But her rivets were clinched by a wiser than you,
  And our sins cannot push the Lord's right hand
    from under.
Better one honest man who can wait for God's
    mind
  In our poor shifting scene here, though heroes
    were plenty!
Better one bite, at forty, of Truth's bitter rind,
  Than the hot wine that gushed from the vintage
    of twenty!

I see it all now: when I wanted a king,
  'T was the kingship that failed in myself I was
      seeking, —
'T is so much less easy to do than to sing,
  So much simpler to reign by a proxy than *be* king!
Yes, I think I *do* see: after all's said and sung,
  Take this one rule of life and you never will
      rue it, —
'T is but do your own duty and hold your own
      tongue,
  And Blondel were royal himself, if he knew it!

MEMORIÆ POSITUM.

R. G. S.

I.

Beneath the trees,
  My life-long friends in this dear spot,
Sad now for eyes that see them not
  I hear the autumnal breeze
Wake the sear leaves to sigh for gladness gone,
Whispering hoarse presage of oblivion, —
  Hear, restless as the seas,
Time's grim feet rustling through the withered grace
Of many a spreading realm and strong-stemmed race,
  Even as my own through these.

  Why make we moan
    For loss that doth enrich us yet
    With upward yearnings of regret?
  Bleaker than unmossed stone
Our lives were but for this immortal gain

Of unstilled longing and inspiring pain!
    As thrills of long-hushed tone
Live in the viol, so our souls grow fine
With keen vibrations from the touch divine
    Of noble natures gone.

  'T were indiscreet
To vex the shy and sacred grief
With harsh obtrusions of relief;
    Yet, Verse, with noiseless feet,
Go whisper: "*This* death hath far choicer ends
Than slowly to impearl in hearts of friends;
    These obsequies 't is meet
Not to seclude in closets of the heart,
But, church-like, with wide doorways, to impart
    Even to the heedless street."

II.

  Brave, good, and true,
I see him stand before me now,
And read again on that young brow,
  Where every hope was new,

How sweet were life! Yet, by the mouth firm-set,
And look made up for Duty's utmost debt,
    I could divine he knew
That death within the sulphurous hostile lines,
In the mere wreck of nobly-pitched designs,
    Plucks heart's-ease, and not rue.

    Happy their end
  Who vanish down life's evening stream
  Placid as swans that drift in dream
    Round the next river-bend!
Happy long life, with honor at the close,
Friends' painless tears, the softened thought of foes!
    And yet, like him, to spend
All at a gush, keeping our first faith sure
From mid-life's doubt and eld's contentment poor, —
    What more could Fortune send?

    Right in the van,
  On the red rampart's slippery swell,
  With heart that beat a charge, he fell
    Foeward, as fits a man;

But the high soul burns on to light men's feet
Where death for noble ends makes dying sweet;
    His life her crescent's span
Orbs full with share in their undarkening days
Who ever climbed the battailous steeps of praise
    Since valor's praise began.

III.

    His life's expense
  Hath won for him coeval youth
  With the immaculate prime of Truth;
    While we, who make pretence.
At living on, and wake and eat and sleep,
And life's stale trick by repetition keep,
    Our fickle permanence
(A poor leaf-shadow on a brook, whose play
Of busy idlesse ceases with our day)
    Is the mere cheat of sense.

    We bide our chance,
  Unhappy, and make terms with Fate
  A little more to let us wait;
    He leads for aye the advance,

Hope's forlorn-hopes that plant the desperate good
For nobler Earths and days of manlier mood;
    Our wall of circumstance
Cleared at a bound, he flashes o'er the fight,
A saintly shape of fame, to cheer the right
    And steel each wavering glance.

    I write of one,
  While with dim eyes I think of three;
  Who weeps not others fair and brave as he?
    Ah, when the fight is won,
Dear Land, whom triflers now make bold to scorn,
(Thee! from whose forehead Earth awaits her
    morn,)
    How nobler shall the sun
Flame in thy sky, how braver breathe thy air,
That thou bred'st children who for thee could dare
    And die as thine have done!

1863.

ON BOARD THE '76.

WRITTEN FOR MR. BRYANT'S SEVENTIETH BIRTHDAY.

NOVEMBER 3, 1864.

OUR ship lay tumbling in an angry sea,
   Her rudder gone, her main-mast o'er the side;
Her scuppers, from the waves' clutch staggering free
   Trailed threads of priceless crimson through the tide;
Sails, shrouds, and spars with pirate cannon torn,
   We lay, awaiting morn.

Awaiting morn, such morn as mocks despair;
   And she that bore the promise of the world
Within her sides, now hopeless, helmless, bare,
   At random o'er the wildering waters hurled;
The reek of battle drifting slow alee
   Not sullener than we.

Morn came at last to peer into our woe,
  When lo, a sail! Now surely help was nigh;
The red cross flames aloft, Christ's pledge; but no,
  Her black guns grinning hate, she rushes by
And hails us:—"Gains the leak? Ay, so we
    thought!
  Sink, then, with curses fraught!"

I leaned against my gun still angry-hot,
  And my lids tingled with the tears held back;
This scorn methought was crueller than shot;
  The manly death-grip in the battle-wrack,
Yard-arm to yard-arm, were more friendly far
    Than such fear-smothered war.

There our foe wallowed, like a wounded brute
  The fiercer for his hurt. What now were best?
Once more tug bravely at the peril's root,
  Though death came with it? Or evade the test
If right or wrong in this God's world of ours
    Be leagued with higher powers?

Some, faintly loyal, felt their pulses lag
  With the slow beat that doubts and then despairs;
Some, caitiff, would have struck the starry flag
  That knits us with our past, and makes us heirs
Of deeds high-hearted as were ever done
    'Neath the all-seeing sun.

But there was one, the Singer of our crew,
  Upon whose head Age waved his peaceful sign,
But whose red heart's-blood no surrender knew;
  And couchant under brows of massive line,
The eyes, like guns beneath a parapet,
    Watched, charged with lightnings yet.

The voices of the hills did his obey;
  The torrents flashed and tumbled in his song;
He brought our native fields from far away,
  Or set us 'mid the innumerable throng
Of dateless woods, or where we heard the calm
    Old homestead's evening psalm.

But now he sang of faith to things unseen,
  Of freedom's birthright given to us in trust;

And words of doughty cheer he spoke between,
  That made all earthly fortune seem as dust,
Matched with that duty, old as Time and new,
  Of being brave and true.

We, listening, learned what makes the might of
    words, —
  Manhood to back them, constant as a star;
His voice rammed home our cannon, edged our
    swords,
  And sent our boarders shouting; shroud and spar
Heard him and stiffened; the sails heard, and wooed
  The winds with loftier mood.

In our dark hours he manned our guns again;
  Remanned ourselves from his own manhood's
    store;
Pride, honor, country, throbbed through all his
    strain;
  And shall we praise? God's praise was his
    before;
And on our futile laurels he looks down,
  Himself our bravest crown.

ODE RECITED AT THE HARVARD COMMEMORATION.

JULY 21, 1865.

I.

WEAK-WINGED is song,
    Nor aims at that clear-ethered height
Whither the brave deed climbs for light:
    We seem to do them wrong,
Bringing our robin's-leaf to deck their hearse
Who in warm life-blood wrote their nobler verse,
Our trivial song to honor those who come
With ears attuned to strenuous trump and drum,
And shaped in squadron-strophes their desire,
Live battle-odes whose lines were steel and fire:
    Yet sometimes feathered words are strong,
A gracious memory to buoy up and save
From Lethe's dreamless ooze, the common grave
    Of the unventurous throng.

II.

To-day our Reverend Mother welcomes back
   Her wisest Scholars, those who understood
The deeper teaching of her mystic tome,
   And offered their fresh lives to make it good:
      No lore of Greece or Rome,
No science peddling with the names of things,
Or reading stars to find inglorious fates,
      Can lift our life with wings
Far from Death's idle gulf that for the many waits,
      And lengthen out our dates
With that clear fame whose memory sings
In manly hearts to come, and nerves them and dilates:
Nor such thy teaching, Mother of us all!
     Not such the trumpet-call
     Of thy diviner mood,
     That could thy sons entice
From happy homes and toils, the fruitful nest
Of those half-virtues which the world calls best,
     Into War's tumult rude;

But rather far that stern device
The sponsors chose that round thy cradle stood
   In the dim, unventured wood,
   The VERITAS that lurks beneath
   The letter's unprolific sheath,
  Life of whate'er makes life worth living,
Seed-grain of high emprise, immortal food,
  One heavenly thing whereof earth hath the giving.

III.

Many loved Truth, and lavished life's best oil
  Amid the dust of books to find her,
Content at last, for guerdon of their toil,
  With the cast mantle she hath left behind her.
   Many in sad faith sought for her,
   Many with crossed hands sighed for her;
   But these, our brothers, fought for her,
   At life's dear peril wrought for her,
   So loved her that they died for her,
   Tasting the raptured fleetness
   Of her divine completeness:
    Their higher instinct knew

Those love her best who to themselves are true,
And what they dare to dream of dare to do;
    They followed her and found her
    Where all may hope to find,
Not in the ashes of the burnt-out mind,
But beautiful, with danger's sweetness round her;
    Where faith made whole with deed
    Breathes its awakening breath
    Into the lifeless creed,
    They saw her plumed and mailed,
    With sweet stern face unveiled,
And all-repaying eyes, look proud on them in death.

IV.

Our slender life runs rippling by, and glides
    Into the silent hollow of the past;
        What is there that abides
    To make the next age better for the last?
        Is earth too poor to give us
    Something to live for here that shall outlive
        us?
    Some more substantial boon

Than such as flows and ebbs with Fortune's fickle
       moon?
     The little that we see
     From doubt is never free;
     The little that we do
     Is but half-nobly true;
     With our laborious hiving
What men call treasure, and the gods call dross,
  Life seems a jest of Fate's contriving,
  Only secure in every one's conniving,
A long account of nothings paid with loss,
Where we poor puppets, jerked by unseen wires,
  After our little hour of strut and rave,
With all our pasteboard passions and desires,
Loves, hates, ambitions, and immortal fires,
  Are tossed pell-mell together in the grave.
  But stay! no age was e'er degenerate,
  Unless men held it at too cheap a rate,
  For in our likeness still we shape our fate;
     Ah, there is something here
  Unfathomed by the cynic's sneer,
  Something that gives our feeble light

A high immunity from Night,
Something that leaps life's narrow bars
To claim its birthright with the hosts of heaven;
   A seed of sunshine that doth leaven
Our earthly dulness with the beams of stars,
      And glorify our clay
With light from fountains elder than the Day;
   A conscience more divine than we,
   A gladness fed with secret tears,
   A vexing, forward-reaching sense
   Of some more noble permanence;
      A light across the sea,
Which haunts the soul and will not let it be,
Still glimmering from the heights of undegenerate
      years.

v.

   Whither leads the path
   To ampler fates that leads?
   Not down through flowery meads,
   To reap an aftermath
   Of youth's vainglorious weeds,
   But up the steep, amid the wrath

And shock of deadly-hostile creeds,
　　Where the world's best hope and stay
By battle's flashes gropes a desperate way,
And every turf the fierce foot clings-to bleeds.
　　Peace hath her not ignoble wreath,
　　Ere yet the sharp, decisive word
Light the black lips of cannon, and the sword
　　　Dreams in its easeful sheath;
But some day the live coal behind the thought,
　　　Whether from Baäl's stone obscene,
　　　Or from the shrine serene
　　　Of God's pure altar brought,
Bursts up in flame; the war of tongue and pen
Learns with what deadly purpose it was fraught,
And, helpless in the fiery passion caught,
Shakes all the pillared state with shock of men:
Some day the soft Ideal that we wooed
Confronts us fiercely, foe-beset, pursued,
And cries reproachful: "Was it, then, my praise,
And not myself was loved? Prove now thy truth;
I claim of thee the promise of thy youth;
Give me thy life, or cower in empty phrase,

The victim of thy genius, not its mate!"
  Life may be given in many ways,
  And loyalty to Truth be sealed
As bravely in the closet as the field,
    So bountiful is Fate;
    But then to stand beside her,
    When craven churls deride her,
To front a lie in arms and not to yield,
    This shows, methinks, God's plan
    And measure of a stalwart man,
    Limbed like the old heroic breeds,
    Who stands self-poised on manhood's solid earth,
  Not forced to frame excuses for his birth,
Fed from within with all the strength he needs.

VI.

Such was he, our Martyr-Chief,
  Whom late the Nation he had led,
  With ashes on her head,
Wept with the passion of an angry grief:
Forgive me, if from present things I turn

To speak what in my heart will beat and burn,
And hang my wreath on his world-honored urn.
    Nature, they say, doth dote,
    And cannot make a man
    Save on some worn-out plan,
    Repeating us by rote:
For him her Old World moulds aside she threw,
    And, choosing sweet clay from the breast
    Of the unexhausted West,
With stuff untainted shaped a hero new,
Wise, steadfast in the strength of God, and true.
    How beautiful to see
Once more a shepherd of mankind indeed,
Who loved his charge, but never loved to lead;
One whose meek flock the people joyed to be,
    Not lured by any cheat of birth,
    But by his clear-grained human worth,
And brave old wisdom of sincerity!
    They knew that outward grace is dust;
    They could not choose but trust
In that sure-footed mind's unfaltering skill,
    And supple-tempered will

That bent like perfect steel to spring again and
 thrust.
His was no lonely mountain-peak of mind,
Thrusting to thin air o'er our cloudy bars,
A sea-mark now, now lost in vapors blind;
Broad prairie rather, genial, level-lined,
Fruitful and friendly for all human kind,
Yet also nigh to Heaven and loved of loftiest
 stars.
 Nothing of Europe here,
Or, then, of Europe fronting mornward still,
 Ere any names of Serf and Peer
 Could Nature's equal scheme deface;
 Here was a type of the true elder race,
And one of Plutarch's men talked with us face to
 face.
 I praise him not; it were too late;
And some innative weakness there must be
In him who condescends to victory
Such as the Present gives, and cannot wait,
 Safe in himself as in a fate.
 So always firmly he:

He knew to bide his time,
And can his fame abide,
Still patient in his simple faith sublime,
Till the wise years decide.
Great captains, with their guns and drums,
Disturb our judgment for the hour,
But at last silence comes;
These all are gone, and, standing like a tower,
Our children shall behold his fame,
The kindly-earnest, brave, foreseeing man,
Sagacious, patient, dreading praise, not blame,
New birth of our new soil, the first American.

VII.

Long as man's hope insatiate can discern
Or only guess some more inspiring goal
Outside of Self, enduring as the pole,
Along whose course the flying axles burn
Of spirits bravely-pitched, earth's manlier brood;
Long as below we cannot find
The meed that stills the inexorable mind;
So long this faith to some ideal Good,

Under whatever mortal names it masks,
   Freedom, Law, Country, this ethereal mood
That thanks the Fates for their severer tasks,
   Feeling its challenged pulses leap,
   While others skulk in subterfuges cheap,
And, set in Danger's van, has all the boon it asks,
   Shall win man's praise and woman's love,
   Shall be a wisdom that we set above
All other skills and gifts to culture dear,
   A virtue round whose forehead we inwreathe
   Laurels that with a living passion breathe
When other crowns grow, while we twine them, sear.
   What brings us thronging these high rites to pay,
   And seal these hours the noblest of our year,
   Save that our brothers found this better way?

VIII.

We sit here in the Promised Land
   That flows with Freedom's honey and milk;
   But 't was they won it, sword in hand,
Making the nettle danger soft for us as silk.

We welcome back our bravest and our best; —
Ah me! not all! some come not with the rest,
Who went forth brave and bright as any here!
I strive to mix some gladness with my strain,
    But the sad strings complain,
    And will not please the ear;
I sweep them for a pæan, but they wane
    Again and yet again
Into a dirge, and die away in pain.
In these brave ranks I only see the gaps,
Thinking of dear ones whom the dumb turf wraps,
Dark to the triumph which they died to gain:
    Fitlier may others greet the living,
    For me the past is unforgiving;
    I with uncovered head
    Salute the sacred dead,
Who went, and who return not. — Say not so!
'T is not the grapes of Canaan that repay,
But the high faith that failed not by the way;
Virtue treads paths that end not in the grave;
No ban of endless night exiles the brave;
    And to the saner mind

We rather seem the dead that stayed behind.
Blow, trumpets, all your exultations blow!
For never shall their aureoled presence lack:
I see them muster in a gleaming row,
With ever-youthful brows that nobler show;
We find in our dull road their shining track;
    In every nobler mood
We feel the orient of their spirit glow,
Part of our life's unalterable good,
Of all our saintlier aspiration;
    They come transfigured back,
Secure from change in their high-hearted ways,
Beautiful evermore, and with the rays
Of morn on their white Shields of Expectation!

IX.

    But is there hope to save
  Even this ethereal essence from the grave?
  What ever 'scaped Oblivion's subtle wrong
Save a few clarion names, or golden threads of
    song?
    Before my musing eye

The mighty ones of old sweep by,
Disvoicëd now and insubstantial things,
As noisy once as we; poor ghosts of kings,
Shadows of empire wholly gone to dust,
And many races, nameless long ago,
To darkness driven by that imperious gust
Of ever-rushing Time that here doth blow:
O visionary world, condition strange,
Where naught abiding is but only Change,
Where the deep-bolted stars themselves still shift
   and range!
Shall we to more continuance make pretence?
Renown builds tombs; a life-estate is Wit;
  And, bit by bit,
The cunning years steal all from us but woe;
 Leaves are we, whose decays no harvest sow.
  But, when we vanish hence,
Shall they lie forceless in the dark below,
Save to make green their little length of sods,
Or deepen pansies for a year or two,
Who now to us are shining-sweet as gods?
Was dying all they had the skill to do?

That were not fruitless: but the Soul resents
Such short-lived service, as if blind events
Ruled without her, or earth could so endure;
She claims a more divine investiture
Of longer tenure than Fame's airy rents;
Whate'er she touches doth her nature share;
Her inspiration haunts the ennobled air,
    Gives eyes to mountains blind,
Ears to the deaf earth, voices to the wind,
And her clear trump sings succor everywhere
By lonely bivouacs to the wakeful mind;
For soul inherits all that soul could dare:
    Yea, Manhood hath a wider span
And larger privilege of life than man.
The single deed, the private sacrifice,
So radiant now through proudly-hidden tears,
Is covered up erelong from mortal eyes
With thoughtless drift of the deciduous years;
But that high privilege that makes all men
    peers,
That leap of heart whereby a people rise
    Up to a noble anger's height,

And, flamed on by the Fates, not shrink, but
grow more bright,
That swift validity in noble veins,
Of choosing danger and disdaining shame,
Of being set on flame
By the pure fire that flies all contact base,
But wraps its chosen with angelic might,
These are imperishable gains,
Sure as the sun, medicinal as light,
These hold great futures in their lusty reins
And certify to earth a new imperial race.

x.

Who now shall sneer?
Who dare again to say we trace
Our lines to a plebeian race?
Roundhead and Cavalier!
Dumb are those names erewhile in battle loud;
Dream-footed as the shadow of a cloud,
They flit across the ear:
That is best blood that hath most iron in 't
To edge resolve with, pouring without stint

    For what makes manhood dear.
    Tell us not of Plantagenets,
Hapsburgs, and Guelfs, whose thin bloods crawl
Down from some victor in a border-brawl!
    How poor their outworn coronets,
Matched with one leaf of that plain civic wreath
Our brave for honor's blazon shall bequeath,
    Through whose desert a rescued Nation sets
Her heel on treason, and the trumpet hears
Shout victory, tingling Europe's sullen ears
    With vain resentments and more vain regrets!

XI.

    Not in anger, not in pride,
    Pure from passion's mixture rude
    Ever to base earth allied,
    But with far-heard gratitude,
    Still with heart and voice renewed,
To heroes living and dear martyrs dead,
The strain should close that consecrates our brave.
    Lift the heart and lift the head!
    Lofty be its mood and grave,

Not without a martial ring,
Not without a prouder tread
And a peal of exultation:
Little right has he to sing
Through whose heart in such an hour
Beats no march of conscious power,
Sweeps no tumult of elation!
'T is no Man we celebrate,
By his country's victories great,
A hero half, and half the whim of Fate,
But the pith and marrow of a Nation
Drawing force from all her men,
Highest, humblest, weakest, all,
For her time of need, and then
Pulsing it again through them,
Till the basest can no longer cower,
Feeling his soul spring up divinely tall,
Touched but in passing by her mantle-hem.
Come back, then, noble pride, for 't is her dower!
How could poet ever tower,
If his passions, hopes, and fears,
If his triumphs and his tears,

Kept not measure with his people?
Boom, cannon, boom to all the winds and waves!
Clash out, glad bells, from every rocking steeple!
Banners, adance with triumph, bend your staves!
    And from every mountain-peak
    Let beacon-fire to answering beacon speak,
    Katahdin tell Monadnock, Whiteface he,
And so leap on in light from sea to sea,
    Till the glad news be sent
    Across a kindling continent,
Making earth feel more firm and air breathe braver:
"Be proud! for she is saved, and all have helped to save her!
She that lifts up the manhood of the poor,
She of the open soul and open door,
With room about her hearth for all mankind!
The fire is dreadful in her eyes no more;
From her bold front the helm she doth unbind,
Sends all her handmaid armies back to spin,
And bids her navies, that so lately hurled
Their crashing battle, hold their thunders in,

Swimming like birds of calm along the un-
harmful shore.
No challenge sends she to the elder world,
That looked askance and hated; a light scorn
Plays o'er her mouth, as round her mighty knees
She calls her children back, and waits the morn
Of nobler day, enthroned between her subject
seas."

XII.

Bow down, dear Land, for thou hast found release!
  Thy God, in these distempered days,
  Hath taught thee the sure wisdom of His ways,
And through thine enemies hath wrought thy peace!
  Bow down in prayer and praise!
No poorest in thy borders but may now
Lift to the juster skies a man's enfranchised brow.
O Beautiful! my Country! ours once more!
Smoothing thy gold of war-dishevelled hair
O'er such sweet brows as never other wore,
  And letting thy set lips,
  Freed from wrath's pale eclipse,

The rosy edges of their smile lay bare,
What words divine of lover or of poet
Could tell our love and make thee know it,
Among the Nations bright beyond compare?
    What were our lives without thee?
    What all our lives to save thee?
    We reck not what we gave thee;
    We will not dare to doubt thee,
But ask whatever else, and we will dare!

L'ENVOI.

TO THE MUSE.

WHITHER? Albeit I follow fast,
   In all life's circuit I but find,
Not where thou art, but where thou wast,
   Sweet beckoner, more fleet than wind!
I haunt the pine-dark solitudes,
   With soft brown silence carpeted,
And plot to snare thee in the woods:
   Peace I o'ertake, but thou art fled!
I find the rock where thou didst rest,
The moss thy skimming foot hath prest;
   All Nature with thy parting thrills,
Like branches after birds new-flown;
   Thy passage hill and hollow fills
With hints of virtue not their own;
In dimples still the water slips
Where thou hast dipt thy finger-tips;

Just, just beyond, forever burn
Gleams of a grace without return;
Upon thy shade I plant my foot,
And through my frame strange raptures shoot;
All of thee but thyself I grasp;
I seem to fold thy luring shape,
And vague air to my bosom clasp,
Thou lithe, perpetual Escape!

One mask and then another drops,
And thou art secret as before:
Sometimes with flooded ear I list,
And hear thee, wondrous organist,
From mighty continental stops
A thunder of new music pour;
Through pipes of earth and air and stone
Thy inspiration deep is blown;
Through mountains, forests, open downs,
Lakes, railroads, prairies, states, and towns,
Thy gathering fugue goes rolling on
From Maine to utmost Oregon;
The factory-wheels in cadence hum,

From brawling parties concords come;
All this I hear, or seem to hear,
But when, enchanted, I draw near
To mate with words the various theme,
Life seems a whiff of kitchen steam,
History an organ-grinder's thrum,
   For thou hast slipt from it and me
And all thine organ-pipes left dumb,
   Most mutable Perversity!

Not weary yet, I still must seek,
And hope for luck next day, next week;
I go to see the great man ride,
Shiplike, the swelling human tide
That floods to bear him into port,
Trophied from Senate-hall and Court;
Thy magnetism, I feel it there,
Thy rhythmic presence fleet and rare,
Making the Mob a moment fine
With glimpses of their own Divine,
As in their demigod they see
   Their cramped ideal soaring free;

'T was thou didst bear the fire about,
  That, like the springing of a mine
Sent up to heaven the street-long shout;
Full well I know that thou wast here,
It was thy breath that brushed my ear;
But vainly in the stress and whirl
I dive for thee, the moment's pearl.

Through every shape thou well canst run,
Proteus, 'twixt rise and set of sun,
Well pleased with logger-camps in Maine
  As where Milan's pale Duomo lies
A stranded glacier on the plain,
  Its peaks and pinnacles of ice
  Melted in many a quaint device,
And sees, above the city's din,
Afar its silent Alpine kin:
I track thee over carpets deep
To wealth's and beauty's inmost keep;
Across the sand of bar-room floors
'Mid the stale reek of boosing boors;
Where drowse the hay-field's fragrant heats,

Or the flail-heart of Autumn beats;
I dog thee through the market's throngs
To where the sea with myriad tongues
Laps the green edges of the pier,
And the tall ships that eastward steer,
Curtsey their farewells to the town,
O'er the curved distance lessening down;
I follow allwhere for thy sake,
Touch thy robe's hem, but ne'er o'ertake,
Find where, scarce yet unmoving, lies,
Warm from thy limbs, thy last disguise;
But thou another shape hast donned,
And lurest still just, just beyond!

But here a voice, I know not whence,
Thrills clearly through my inward sense,
Saying: "See where she sits at home
While thou in search of her dost roam!
All summer long her ancient wheel
  Whirls humming by the open door,
Or, when the hickory's social zeal
  Sets the wide chimney in a roar,

TO THE MUSE.

Close-nestled by the tinkling hearth,
It modulates the household mirth
With that sweet serious undertone
Of duty, music all her own;
Still as of old she sits and spins
Our hopes, our sorrows, and our sins;
With equal care she twines the fates
Of cottages and mighty states;
She spins the earth, the air, the sea,
The maiden's unschooled fancy free,
The boy's first love, the man's first grief,
The budding and the fall o' the leaf;
The piping west-wind's snowy care
For her their cloudy fleeces spare,
Or from the thorns of evil times
She can glean wool to twist her rhymes;
Morning and noon and eve supply
To her their fairest tints for dye,
But ever through her twirling thread
There spires one line of warmest red,
Tinged from the homestead's genial heart,
The stamp and warrant of her art;

With this Time's sickle she outwears,
And blunts the Sisters' baffled shears.

"Harass her not: thy heat and stir
But greater coyness breed in her;
Yet thou mayst find, ere Age's frost,
Thy long apprenticeship not lost,
Learning at last that Stygian Fate
Unbends to him that knows to wait.
The Muse is womanish, nor deigns
Her love to him that pules and plains;
With proud, averted face she stands
To him that wooes with empty hands.
Make thyself free of Manhood's guild;
Pull down thy barns and greater build;
The wood, the mountain, and the plain
Wave breast-deep with the poet's grain;
Pluck thou the sunset's fruit of gold,
Glean from the heavens and ocean old;
From fireside lone and trampling street
Let thy life garner daily wheat;
The epic of a man rehearse,

Be something better than thy verse;
Make thyself rich, and then the Muse
Shall court thy precious interviews,
Shall take thy head upon her knee,
And such enchantment lilt to thee,
That thou shalt hear the life-blood flow
From farthest stars to grass-blades low,
And find the Listener's science still
Transcends the Singer's deepest skill!"

THE END.

www.ingramcontent.com/pod-product-compliance
Lightning Source LLC
Chambersburg PA
CBHW031343230426
43670CB00006B/423